The Unfaithful Widow

Enjoy the book!
Barbara
Barth

Dedicated To
The Power Of Love

The Unfaithful Widow

Fragmented Memoirs
Of My First Year Alone

By
Barbara Barth

Outskirts Press, Inc.
Denver, Colorado

Outskirts Press, Inc.
http://www.outskirtspress.com

ISBN: 978-1-4327-5075-6

Outskirts Press and the "OP" logo are trademarks belonging to Outskirts Press, Inc.

PRINTED IN THE UNITED STATES OF AMERICA

A Note From The Author:

I refer to my husband as "my husband" throughout my book. However, we lived together for twenty years and were married another five. So when I talk about *us* we are either living blissfully in sin or happily married. I'll leave it to you to sort it out.

I have not changed the names to protect the innocent. No names needed. There *are* some very bad dates. You'll know who you are.

It is not a senior moment on my part that my friends and family are not called by their names, but rather they are in my story by the place they hold in my heart.

The dogs insisted that I use their names. There is a pecking order in this household and the dogs tell me what to do. They are such publicity hounds.

I thought my old life would go on forever. The biggest shock of all was that it changed. My husband used to kid that I hated change of any kind. I was a nester. I had my job for 36 years and my husband for 25. Change smacked me right between the eyes just as I was turning sixty. My life and my self-image were gone in a heartbeat.

So here I am. Essays, vignettes, and other assorted fragmented thoughts on my first year alone. Proof that life does go on and can be good again. I've discovered if you put enough stuff out to the universe, the universe will bring you what you need. It's making that first step that counts.

I still tell my husband, *I love you.* I look in the mirror every morning and say, *I love you too.* Meaning me. I'm laughing again. A lot.

A round of applause for my sis, Pam, *Pam King Photography* and her friend Jill, *Jill Applegate Design* for their help with my book. Pam's back cover photomontage of the hellhounds and me is my very favorite portrait. Oh to be that thin. She also designed the inside altered art photos. Jill heard my story and designed my book cover. She hit it right on. I love it.

And *Mama Mia*, who is the sexy lady in those photos, the one in the bikini and driving off into the sunset at the end? You may have guessed it. *My Mom.* She is an inspiration for all things good.

Contents

Definitions

Widow:
a woman whose spouse has died.

Unfaithful:
Not true to one's spouse.

Conundrum:
A riddle in which the
answer makes a play on words.

Prologue

My Other Car Is A Corvette

I see those bumper stickers all the time on old cars and trucks, you know the one that tells you their other car is a gem of a sports car. I used to smile and think, *yeah, right*. Well, now I am one of those people. My 1995 Honda van has a bumper sticker telling the world my other car is a Corvette. *And it is*. I wonder if anyone takes that seriously?

Of all people, I am the last one you would imagine buying a Corvette. Cars have never interested me. But a 1979 Corvette Stingray found me through a dating service a few months after my husband's death just as I turned that dreaded sixty. When a long, sleek sports car in great shape makes that kind of a pass at you, what's a gal to do? I cashed out a money market account and threw caution to the wind. That car had to be mine.

It has T-tops you can remove on glorious days and let the wind blow through your hair. My vintage cat eye sunglasses are tucked in the visor ready at any given moment I want to hit the road. It is a car that reminds me it is great to be alive. Buying that car put me back in the driver's seat of my life. I rarely travel far from home, but when I sit in that car I am a million miles away.

Now that I own one I've discovered everyone has a Corvette fantasy.

"Oh my God, a vintage Corvette, I love that car." An old friend from my high school days got back in touch with me this past year. He swooned when I sent him a photo of my car.

"You know I was saving to buy one all those years ago, but used the money for my honeymoon instead." He's been married forty years to the same gal. "Made the better choice," he chuckled remembering the young gal he had married so long ago. "Think of me when you drive it."

My car purchase tickled those close to me. Shocking to them as it was so out of character for me. "You go girl." I had several of those messages on voice mail.

The car became an urban legend with my friends. It took two weeks for the repairs to be completed before I drove the 40 miles to bring it home. No one had seen my Corvette, but the stories about my purchase hit the phone lines before my car hit the driveway.

The car eased me into my journey to find a new life for myself. A boost to my confidence, something bright to talk about, and a hell of a ride on my bumpy road to whatever lurked ahead.

It has my back when people I don't know well get too nosey about my loss. As they look sadly at me I smile at them. "Did I tell you about my Corvette?" Talk about changing gears mid sentence.

I like to think the car and I have a lot in common. *Not new, not old, but stylishly vintage.* It was well loved and taken care of by a previous owner. You can tell by the shape it's in. The same with me. I was well loved. The shape I'm in, my own doing.

The other night at a book club meeting we were discussing writing from the female experience. Someone suggested, "Why don't we each write about something personal in our lives and make our own book."

My best friend burst out with, "Barbara just finished her book."

All eyes turned to me since this information came out of the blue.

"What's your book about?" I could see I had become the center of attention.

"A memoir of my first year as a widow."

Now that I've said it out loud I am nervous. So far the book has been mine alone, my story private except for a few close friends and family members. How would others view my year? The way I chose to save myself has raised a few eyebrows. I hate to be judged and my way of dealing with things can open a can of worms.

"You started dating three months after your husband died?" That was the first tough question tossed at me. A few of the ladies turned to each other and started whispering something I could not hear.

Then they looked back at me. "Did you meet someone you wanted to date so quickly or did you just decide to get out and play around?"

God, how I hate that question.

Read my book. You'll understand. I thought it, but left it unsaid.

I stared at my best friend wanting to kick her for letting the cat out of the bag. She was laughing at the situation and rolling her eyes in my direction. She's right, you know. I should be laughing too. I made it through the worst year of my life and can smile. So I did what I always do when others poke at me and get on my nerves. I ask that question that changes the conversation in a heartbeat.

"Do you know my other car is a Corvette?"

Spring

I Used To Have A Handle On Life, But It Broke.

Confessions Of
The Unfaithful Widow

How would my husband feel about my dating? I don't have a clue. In all our years together we never discussed life's big issues. We were rarely apart and I was active in his business, but we never agreed on how things should be done.

Some years back while we were watching TV, eating popcorn, and having a fun quiet evening I looked at my husband and said, "I wonder why we never had children?" It was really more of a comment brought on by the show we were watching, but his answer surprised me.

"We never talked about it."

He was right. Good thing we agreed we were meant for each other. It was a wonder we finally talked about getting married and did.

We never talked about what we would do if one of us died and of course, when he became so ill, I could not even approach the subject of death. I talked of hope.

But over the years I would poke at him, teasing him on that subject, never expecting I would face a future without him. He came back with only one remark on my silly scenarios.

Since I was an antique dealer and everything I owned could be sold, I'd tell him, "If something happens to me, don't pitch my stuff. Date a dealer who can help you with a sale."

I wanted to decorate with painted primitives and fill the walls with art; he liked modern pieces and clean white walls. So I'd remind him, "I'm going to fill the house with all my furniture and hang paintings everywhere if you leave me."

And because I love dogs and want every stray I see and he was of the philosophy one dog was enough, I'd say, "I'll fill the house with hounds." We did make it to two dogs, but that was a fluke, well organized by me.

He ignored all my comments.

Then one evening after a romp in the bedroom with my handsome husband I kidded him, "God if anything happens to you I'll have to find a young guy. No old one could take your place."

Well that finally got a reply from him.

"I thought there would only be paintings and dogs."

Who knew he had been listening?

"He would want you to be happy." Everyone tells me that. And yes, I know he would. But his definition of happy and mine would have differed as much as our views and opinions differed our entire life.

Does dating now make me the unfaithful widow? I've asked myself that question. No one could have loved him more and you can't be unfaithful to that.

Whether he would agree is another question. Since we never agreed on anything.

Welcome To My World

Becoming a widow right before my 60th birthday was not on my list of things to do. I had a great life, a husband who I adored, retired early from my job with the feds and got to live my fantasy as an antique dealer. I saw my life in Technicolor.

My fondest moment of retirement was the first summer I did the Lakewood Antique Show. Summers in Atlanta are hot and sultry. The monthly show was at the old 1916's fairgrounds south of the city. Dealers came from all over the country to set up in the courtyards and Spanish styled stucco buildings. My space was inside one of those buildings where the only flow of air came from the huge open front and rear doors. The buildings did not have air conditioning. The humidity was so thick it felt like it was clinging to my body. I was hot, sweaty and trying to cool off with my tiny fan. The radio played the Pina Colada song and as I hummed to it I thought *this is the life*. I smiled as I patted my face with a cool cloth thinking how happy I was, how good life was. I thought nothing could ever go wrong.

Well it all went wrong. My husband became ill. It crept up on him slowly and took months to diagnosis. The year that began with everyone thinking he had an allergy ended with him dying of a rare immune system disease.

That last week we had his usual visits to all his doctors. No one was expecting that he would not make it through the week. His disease was playing hell with his body, but he was still up and moving, however slowly. He cooked dinner for my best friend and me on that Sunday.

Wednesday he had me worried, more so than usual. Something was different with him. He had very little sleep the last few days, so maybe that was it I told myself. But I called his doctors and spoke to someone as late as 10PM. He had a doctor's appointment the next morning. All we had to do was make it through the night. Seemed like a simple thing.

He was on the couch in a very fitful sleep, but then he was agitated many nights because of the strong medicines he was taking. Some evenings he would snap out of a deep sleep hallucinating in a world I did not understand. Then in a moment he would be back to normal, that guy I knew and loved.

At 2AM I was increasingly nervous. A panic was building in me.

"Do you know who this is?" I asked him, touching his arm and face.

"Of course, it's Barbara." His response made me relax a little.

An hour later his breathing was steady and he had fallen into a quiet sleep. Exhausted I closed my eyes and drifted off.

In the two hours I was off my watch he left me. I woke to a strange silence in the room and realized he was gone.

I called 911, just like they do in the movies, but this was real life. A life that suddenly did not seem real to me at all. Within a few minutes my driveway was full of vehicles with flashing lights and strangers were in my kitchen trying to get information from me. It was 5AM.

Angels? You tell me. I called my best friend terrified she would be asleep. She turns the bedroom phone off at night. She answered my ring.

"Something woke me up at 4AM and I couldn't get back to sleep," she told me. She had gotten dressed and was downstairs ready to go when my call came to her.

"I'm on my way." The most blessed words I could hear at that moment.

Thank you, I whispered to a higher being.

She arrived quickly and took charge of the funeral home, the police, the invaders of my home.

I made all the calls to family at that ungodly hour when the phone rings and you think the worst. And there I was, calling with the worst.

The dogs knew that something was wrong, and I was amazed at how they handled themselves in those wee morning hours. In all the panic surrounding me, they were my sea of calm. Foxy, my Alpha queen, had to be put into the bedroom as she was trying to run the show. She went quietly to wait for me. Jake, my handicapped ninety-five pound shepherd had pulled himself to the back door and was sitting on the floor, his head cocked as he watched the police write up their report.

"Can you move this dog?" the police asked me.

My best friend and I looked at each other, and it was the one moment I could smile sadly.

"No," I said firmly. "He can't walk and I am not lifting him."

They looked at Jake, shook their heads and continued writing.

Foxy never saw my husband's body leave, but she knew he was gone. Jake watched as my husband was wheeled out and never left his spot by the door. Neither dog outwardly grieved but turned their attention to me. They were my solace in a time when nothing could comfort me.

Family and friends stayed with me the rest of the week and the flurry of activity kept me moving when I wanted to curl up and hide.

My husband was as handsome in death as he had been in life. I said my goodbye at the funeral home. *Damn you for leaving me.* I bent to give him a final kiss. But I knew he went exactly as he would have wanted, his way and before his illness controlled his life.

I never thought I would be alone again, but in those quiet moments on an early spring morning in the skip of a heartbeat my world changed forever.

On Xanax, Zoloft and Margaritas

"*Give the* phone to your mother," my husband's mother almost yelled at me. I handed the phone to my mother, too tired to even ask why. It had been less than 48 hours since my husband died and I was strung out. Too nervous to sleep, pacing and otherwise trying to just move through the day. Friends were pouring through the front door and my family took care of them. I sat there in a daze not really wanting to talk to anyone, but glad for the flurry of activity.

"Call the doctor and get her on some drugs," my mother-in-law advised my mother.

"You know, she's right," my mother agreed. "You need something to help calm you down." I guess they both decided I needed to be medicated. The idea seemed suddenly appealing to me. Maybe I could blot out everything with a pill.

The doctor had me come to his office that day. He gave me two prescriptions. "One is for depression," he explained, "the other is for anxiety." Zoloft and Xanax, my two new best friends.

I filled the prescriptions and headed home to see what fresh hell awaited me.

"The funeral home just called to remind you of your appointment this afternoon," my sis yelled from the kitchen as I came in.

I popped two pills and looked at my mother. "Might as well go now."

I had given the funeral home instructions over the phone so that I wouldn't have to sit and talk about it there. My husband was to be sent to the family plot in Ohio. My mother-in-law was taking charge with the cemetery and ordering his headstone. All I needed to do was sign some papers and leave a check.

A young woman dressed in black greeted us. She had a name, but to me she was *Miss Death*.

"I see you have requested the basic cremate and ship plan." She then pulled a brochure from her desk and with a graceful gesture of her hand continued. "May I show you our upgrades?"

For a minute I had to think, *was I getting a vacation package?* Anger started turning my face red. My mother noticed my expression and placed her hand on my arm. I took a deep breath.

"I think I was specific about what I wanted over the phone. My husband's mother will take care of the rest." I was amazed at my calm. Maybe these drugs were working.

Several days later I went back to pick up the death certificates and something did not look right. It took me a minute to realize that they had my husband's middle name wrong. They had typed *John* instead of *James*. I brought this to their attention.

"Are you sure?" The clerk questioned me. "Do you have anything to prove that?"

Well, I may be on drugs, but I think after 25 years I know my husband's middle name. I smiled politely. "Why, actually I do." I dug into my purse and handed them his driver's license. It would take 24 hours to have the certificates corrected. Hopefully I would never hear from this place again.

My family left after the long weekend and I was on my own, truly on my own, since now this was a household of one. To keep busy I met the girls for lunch, shopped, then came home and went into the sleep of death for hours on the couch.

I called the nurse. "I don't know if these pills are working? All

I do is sleep."

"That's the Xanax, honey," she informed me. "Will make you sleepy. Are you following the instructions?"

"Yes, one every six hours just as the bottle instructed."

"Well, just rest and we'll set up an appointment for you to see the doctor."

I cut back on the Xanax and only used it if I became too stressed. I still took Zoloft each night.

Late June a call came in from a business associate of my husband's. "Going to be in town for a meeting. Let's have lunch and I'll go over some of the paperwork you have questions about."

We had never met in person, but had talked on the phone many times in the month since my husband died. He was younger, married and cute. I remembered a photo he sent my husband earlier that year.

Might be nice to meet him in person, I thought. All I had seen in the last month were faces looking at me with sympathy. A new face might be just what the doctor ordered.

I decided to dress up for our business meeting. I wore my favorite long black skirt, a white linen blouse and of course, my vintage turquoise. I started to get excited, like I was going on a date.

Am I nuts? I wondered. Then the anxiety hit me and I popped a Xanax before I headed to my car.

I walked into the restaurant and saw him immediately. Tall and handsome, just like his photo. He stood up as I approached him and introduced himself. I smiled back at him and thought he looked sexy. As we sat down I handed him a stack of papers I wasn't sure what to do with. While he looked at them I leaned across the table closer to him and softly said, "I think I could use a drink." I was a wreck, he was cute and I needed to steady myself. "A Margarita would be lovely," I added.

We each had one. Halfway through mine I was totally smashed. I looked across at him with the only question I thought was important. "Is there any chance you are getting divorced in the near future?"

He looked at me, folded the papers and dropped them in his brief case. "I'll go over these later and call you."

Then his hand shot up for the waitress. "Two more of these," he told her.

We sat there from one in the afternoon until eight at night. We never ate lunch. But had a great time laughing and drinking. I only had two drinks, but we added extra shots of tequila to the last drink to freshen it up. I could finally relax with someone and I talked my head off.

Did he want to go home with me? I'd like to think so. *Would it have happened if he'd asked?* I don't know. I think I felt at ease with him because he knew my husband. I know I was attracted to him because he made me feel happy for seven hours during a period of my life I had nothing to smile about.

I drove the three miles home high as a kite. The feeling of warmth and laughter kept me company that night, not the young man I flirted so outrageously with.

I like to dream, *what if he were single*? But that is a fantasy brought on by Zoloft, Xanax and Margaritas and the smile of some- one across the table who looked at me as the woman I was, and not the widow I had become.

The Breath Of Life

"Foxy, wake up," I call from across the room. I am sitting on the couch and she is sleeping quietly on the floor by the front window. I start to worry something has happened to her then stop myself from getting up and checking on her.

Relax, she's fine. I reach over for the remote and change channels on the TV. I always have the TV on now. The quiet in the house is spooky. The sound of the drum roll on the late night show wakes Foxy and she trots over to me.

"Good girl." I keep biscuits on the table for this very moment.

I can't put my finger on when it happened, but somewhere in my early fifties I started worrying about breathing. Not my breathing, but the breathing of those I loved. I became obsessed with the thought that someone would stop breathing on me in their sleep.

It began innocently sleeping in bed with my husband. He would snore some nights, let out a loud grunt, and then there was total silence. I would quickly slip my hand under his nose moving it around until I felt his breath on my fingers. As soon as I felt a little puff of air I'd roll over and go back to sleep, satisfied all was well.

Two years before I retired a friend hired my husband to take charge of a small renovation on his house. He wanted to sell the house. It was badly in need of cosmetic work. Then a residential realtor, familiar with the neighborhood, came on site with his hit list.

"Needs a master suite. Have a few other ideas in mind too."

Our friend wanted those changes and the job was escalated. My husband pulled together a crew and was on the site early every morning. He came home exhausted and went to bed too early for me, mistress of the night. I slept in the guest room across the hall from him during those months.

At the midnight hour I would tiptoe down the dark hallway by flashlight, Foxy trotting behind me, hoping we wouldn't make any noises to wake my husband. We would slip quietly into the dark guest room where I would read by flashlight. Foxy liked to sleep on the bed next to me, a treat for her since she usually slept on the floor next to our bed in the main bedroom. I could hear my husband's soft breathing across the hallway and felt as if we were still close together.

I remember one night reading, flashlight in hand, the soft moonlight streaming through the thin lace curtains giving the room an odd glow. My husband let out a horrid noise from across the hall. I put down my book, turned my head towards the door, and waited to hear him stir. Only silence greeted me.

My bare feet quickly hit the floor as I ran in to check on my husband. I had the flashlight in my hand and swung it in his direction. I wanted to be sure he was OK.

"What the hell," he screamed and jumped straight up. Then he looked at me as though I'd lost my mind. "What are you doing? Damn, you scared me." I was lucky I didn't give him a heart attack. The light flashing so quickly pulled him out of a deep sleep and he was pissed.

"Sorry honey." I gave him a kiss while he grumbled and turned to go back to sleep. I pattered back to the guest room smiling he was OK.

The dogs did not escape my obsession either. That same week I surprised my husband Foxy got her share of attention. She snorts when she sleeps. I was dozing off when Foxy let out a loud grunt laying next to me in the guest bed. Then total silence. I gently poked at her in the dark. She didn't move. I whispered, "Foxy." Nothing. I reached out to touch her chest and it seemed so still. Panic hit me. So I did the only thing I could think of. I hauled off and smacked her butt with my hand. Foxy jumped straight up and turned in my direction. "Give me a kiss," I whispered to her, so thrilled she had moved. She came over and gave me one of her little licks, then curled back down to sleep. Dogs have a better attitude about an abrupt wake up call than husbands, I decided.

My other dog Jake had health issues that kept me on edge. So I watched him closely while he was sleeping and if he became too quiet, I'd go over and poke at him, praying he'd move. I couldn't leave it alone.

"Did it again," I confessed to a friend over lunch. "This time Jake. Thought he had stopped breathing he was so still."

"God Barbara, what is it with you?" My friend laughed, teasing me. "You are always checking to see who is breathing. Remind me not to spend the night at your place."

Then it was no longer funny. I found my husband on the sofa that early May morning. He was no longer breathing.

I sometimes wonder if I knew our time would be short. When we met I knew he was the one. Do you believe in souls meeting again? Maybe I lost him too soon in a prior life and that knowledge stayed with me into this life. I don't know what I believe along those lines, but it is something I wonder about on nights when I can't sleep.

I still have moments like tonight with Foxy but I let it pass. *Breathe*, I tell myself. I have stopped worrying what will be and just worry how I will be each day. The things I fear no longer control my life.

I leave the TV on all night. I can see the flickering lights down the hallway from the bedroom and the faint murmurs of sound that travel to me break the total silence in my room.

The sound of my own breathing at night seems louder than all the sounds that filled the air when my husband was sleeping next to me. Those sounds that disturb you while you are trying to sleep but let you know there is someone next to you in the still of the night. My breathing echoes throughout the empty room a constant reminder that I am alone in my bed. Not even the TV can distract from that.

Forever

You learn the true meaning of the word *forever* with the death of a loved one. All other *forevers* are simply warps in time.

I wish you could stay like this forever, a mother holds her first child.

Yuck, this day seems forever, a restless kid sitting in school wants to get out and play.

You are grounded forever, parents are mad at a child who stayed out late at night.

Will he/she stay mad forever? a fight between loved ones.

This diet is taking forever, the scale hasn't moved a pound since yesterday.

God, my company has been here forever, guests who don't know when to leave.

I've been looking for someone like you forever, the perfect mate is found.

Let's make love forever, the sex is so wonderful, you can't get enough.

I will love you forever, as a lifetime together is being planned.

I'll be here forever, a promise from someone who loves you.

Nothing lasts forever, the advice everyone gives to make change acceptable.

All the *forevers* we complain about or are excited about. But the death of a loved one is the real *forever*.

I like to let my mind wander back to the past remembering all its sweetness. I live in the present where it is moment to moment that counts for me now. When I look at the future, the word *forever* is mine for all time.

Letter To God

Dear God,

Am I going to make it? So far I am not sure how I am doing. Being a widow was not in my game plan, but it must be in yours for me. Help me to be a good sport because right now I am not a team player. I am sad, lonely and mad that I am here by myself.

I am tired of crying. I am crying now because I am alone and miss my husband. I cried every night for a year worrying about his health. I guess I am a big crybaby.

I want a good happy life back. I had a life I loved. I don't like this new one. This is the biggest darkest void I have ever been in. I need some light, some news, something to do.

I pray you have some ideas for me that will appear soon. You know me, no patience. The grief is gobbling me up and I need a big plate of courage.

I am counting on you to help me reach the final goal, that being a full life again. The other final goal I hope is way off in the future. I need time to get this right.

Sincerely,
The Widow Barbara

The W Word

I have always hated the word *Widow*. It conjures up the bleakest of images for me. The word makes me think of an old woman, cloaked in black, alone, an empty shell of a person that once was full of life.

Now I am that woman who is a widow.

I look in the mirror. *Do I know you? You seem vaguely familiar.* Then the face turns and I realize it is my face.

I call a good friend. "Do I really look like shit? Be honest."

She is kind. "Honey, you've been through it. You look tired. But you don't look like shit."

That brings a little smile to my face. Good friends lie to you when you need it.

The day I went to see the probate attorney was the day I decided to pull myself together. I wore an ankle length black skirt and T-shirt. I was decked out in my chunky turquoise necklaces and bracelets. I wore my Mary Jane canvas shoes. I sprayed perfume around my head and walked out that door.

Two hours later I left the attorney's office too depressed to go home. So I headed to the antique shop where I have my booth. It seemed the closest and friendliest place I could think of.

"We've never seen you in a skirt," the gal behind the counter remarked and actually clasped her hands in glee. Now there was someone who could perk you up.

"Just back from dealing with the will," I replied and made a sad face. Then I did a full curtsey, dipping and holding out my long skirt.

"My widow's outfit."

I started to relax with the familiarity of the shop and smiled at her.

"Black since I'm a widow and turquoise jewelry 'cause I'm hip." I liked the sound of that.

She was looking strangely at me.

"I am hip, aren't I?" I looked straight at her. She'd better answer that one right.

"The hippest." She grinned at me with that remark. She was forty-five, skinny and lived on the edge. I was the sixty year old widow.

Good answer.

Now that is an image I can start to live with.

There is a huge painting hanging on the wall behind my bed that fills the entire space. I purchased it on Ebay after my husband died. I put in a very high bid, but it seems I was the only one who wanted the painting. It was mine for a song.

It is the profile of an old Amish style woman sitting in her dark dress on the porch of an old house. She is looking out to the blue sea and purple mountains fill the back skyline. There is a small orange bird perched on the top of the wooden porch rail that runs in front of her.

This painting fascinates me as I try to imagine what the artist's intention was. I would love to know the story of the woman. Is she a widow like me or is her husband fishing for the day's catch? Is she waiting for a man who will never return or is she patiently awaiting the arrival of her mate? Her expression is blank as she gazes at the water in front of her so I can't get a handle on her situation. She appears calm. The bird's color is oddly off in its brightness. Is the bird symbolic of hope in a situation that appears hopeless?

I love this painting. I am that solemn woman looking out for a husband who definitely will not return. There is a peacefulness and serenity in the painting that comforts me. The woman is stoic and no matter what her story, she will survive. I smile when I look at her and she has become my friend.

If art imitates life and vice versa, perhaps I will be more like my painting; serene and mysterious and waiting for who knows what to come my way.

Things Not To Say
To A New Widow

Friends and family mean well, but at the time of a loss many don't know what to say and sometimes say the silliest things. Here are my favorites, shoulda, coulda, wish you hadn't said that list. And yes, someone said each to me within the first few weeks of my husband's death. Not really so bad, but at the time all I could think was *why are you saing this now*? My brain was spinning enough without having to filter in these remarks. But some actually got filed away for future use, and the others, well they make me laugh now.

You look so tired.
You need a smaller place. Who will do the maintenance now?
Things happen for a reason.
Gee, your thighs look heavy. Have you gained weight?
Hey, you can do whatever you like now.
It's hard to cook for just one.
Do you want the space next to him in the family plot? But you're
    young and may get married again.
Well, now you can decorate the house the way you want.
The house finally looks lived in.
If my husband died, I'd never want sex again.
Keep a loaded gun in the house. *(For me or the intruders?)*
Let's not forget the remark from the 65 year old man dating his
    45 year old trophy girlfriend, a gal pal of mine from my old

work days. "I walk five miles a day. If you start walking now in a year you'll be back in shape and can start dating." (*And then I can date an ass like you?* I held my tongue).

Have you been to Curves yet?

He was a great guy, but try to find someone with a different personality.

My favorite advice from my husband's best friend; "Get out of your comfort zone and learn to do new things."

Thank you kindly, sir, that is exactly what I am doing.

Down The Rabbit Hole

What is it about time that makes every one cranky? My time that is, when I am running late. I finally arrive, shouldn't that count for something?

Like Alice's *White Rabbit* I am always chiming, "I'm late! I'm late!" The year my husband had his weekly visits to the doctors was the only time I was ever punctual. You know that phrase, *a matter of life and death*. But my life before and since finds me frantically trying to get somewhere just a few minutes later than I should.

I don't plan on being late. I start out with all the good intentions of being on time, then I get distracted. If you know me well, you know not to show up at my house earlier than planned. And then if you are on time, you are lucky if I am ready. If we are going to meet somewhere, be sure to bring a book.

"Come over for dinner tomorrow." I couldn't believe I actually said those words. No one has been in the house other than my best friend since my husband died.

"What are you cooking?"

Obviously this was not a close friend if he asked that question.

"Pizza delivery. Does that work for you?" Now I am sorry I've opened my mouth to take this step.

But the plans were made and my friend was due shortly.

I looked at the floor with its fine layer of dog hairs and then at the clock. *Plenty of time*, I thought. *I'll run the vacuum.* Dog hairs are my social faux pas. It is especially fatal when the person is wearing black.

I had just pulled the vacuum into the living room when there was a loud knock on my front door.

The dogs started barking and I ran up to the door yelling over the howling hounds, "Yes, who is it?"

My guest had arrived early. Another indication this was not someone who knew me well. There I was standing in my knickers and bra.

"Wait a minute, I'll be ready in a jiff."

Well, I thought pleasantly to myself, *no need to vacuum now.*

For weeks after my husband's death the phone rang constantly. Friends calling to see how I was doing and making plans for lunch and dinner. Answering all those calls from caring friends as I was running out the door made me late meeting the friends who had called earlier to make plans.

My best friend and I really never went anywhere together before my husband died. She was my husband's good friend too, his tomboy friend he called her. They loved to watch home remodeling shows on TV. So we just met at our houses to hang out. She's a chef and he loved to cook. So dinner at either home was a treat for me. Who needed to go out for dinner with those two around? On a rare occasion the three of us would head out to see a movie.

That all changed after my husband died. She and I were on our own now. Our first outing as a twosome was a fiasco.

"Yes, I'll be there at noon," I assured her. We were meeting at Goodwill. I hang out at thrift shops and drag all my friends there.

"Did I tell you I got a Coach bag last week? $17.00." I couldn't decide if I was bragging or complaining. I am used to finding designer leather bags for under $3.00.

"But it's a Coach bag. Check out retail prices on those," the kid behind the counter with the spiked yellow hair and pieced ears was excited about the purse. He likes to point out the super deals to me.

Lunch was going to be next on our agenda at a sandwich place nearby. I was looking forward to having some fun. "See you, can't wait. Morning has been a drag."

The phone rang just as I was heading out the door. I reached for it and there was another invitation for lunch. "Love to. Did I tell you what happened when …." Ten minutes later I was driving furiously to catch up with my best friend.

I got to the shop and couldn't find her. She didn't know that when I ran late I'd call from my cell and I didn't know she kept her cell turned off.

I know all the kids who work there. "My friend was to meet me here, did you see her? Tall, short blond hair and probably in slacks and a white shirt."

"Yeah, she was here. Kept walking in and out the door, the reason we noticed her. I think she left."

"Sorry." I called her on my cell, she had just gotten home. "You know, another call came in and I got caught up."

"Don't answer the phone when it rings if you are meeting someone," she lectured me in a kindly manner. "Let it go to voice mail and you'll have something to do later."

I know that sounds easy. But I was lonely in the house and when the phone rang, I wanted to talk. Didn't matter what I was supposed to be doing.

A few days later we decided to try lunch again. The phone rang and I reached for it. My hand was almost to the receiver when I did a u-turn and walked away. I smiled, closed the door behind me and left.

"See how well I did," I teased her since I was actually a few minutes earlier than her at the restaurant.

That night I checked my messages. Out of all the calls that came in over the last few days, the one I did not answer was the cemetery in Ohio needing my release so my mother-in-law could order my husband's head stone. Nothing I could do about it until morning.

So I picked up the phone and called my best friend. "Thanks a lot for the advice, now even the dead are having to wait for me." She got my drift and we both laughed over it.

I have a vision that is my funeral. All my friends are invited to the chapel for a memorial service. My only instruction to my executor is that my casket comes out fifteen minutes after all the guests arrive. I want them to know I left this earth as I lived, running late for a very important date.

Sex, Always On My Mind

Sex. I totally forgot about sex. Which is unusual for me. But today it hit me in the face. *I've lost my sex partner.* How did that not crop up on my list of widow woes until now?

"Do you know I have had regular sex since I was 19?" I called my best friend. I dump everything on her and at all hours.

"That's nice to know before breakfast." She obviously didn't take this as seriously as I did. "I take it you're feeling better?"

"Well, it's a hell of a time to have to start thinking about sex again. What am I going to do?" I was used to doing it, not thinking about it. Big difference.

I asked the same question to my husband's cousin in Indiana.

"Buy a silver bullet and stop worrying about it." She gave me one of her big hearty laughs.

What the hell is a silver bullet? I consider myself to be in the know about sex toys, vibrators. But a silver bullet? I didn't want to look uninformed. I laughed back in agreement. "You're right, should have thought of that myself."

"Yep, hon, it will be the best date around."

That night I Googled *silver bullet.* A zippy mini compact vibrator. Just what every gal needs the website advised. Much different than the larger ones I've always seen. *Hmmm, should I put one on my Christmas list?*

Sex was part of my routine for 25 years with one man. Didn't have to give it much thought. Any night, or day for that matter, could be full of *hot sex, fun sex, or no sex at all.* As natural as any other activity I did. I liked to call it sex-on-demand. Now all I have is cable.

Bummer.

Sex has always been on my mind. I was sure curious about it as a teenager. I was raised you got married first. I knew some of my friends were *doing it* and I was in awe of them. Truth be, I had no idea what that meant.

One summer right after high school my sis and I were allowed to go to Panama City for a weekend at the beach without our parents. We met some new friends for dinner than afterwards I snuck out to meet a guy a little older than me for a late night walk on the beach. He knew about my earlier dinner date. We strolled along until we found a nice quiet spot, dropped a blanket and sat down. When he made his move to kiss me I thought I would discourage him. "No thanks. I've already had my sex for tonight."

God does look after fools. *Silly me*. I thought you could only have sex once in a night. As I got older and *finally had sex* I realized I was able to have it more than once a night, but sometimes my partner couldn't. Tsk. Tsk.

The guy realized I had no clue. He jumped up doing a little jig. Then he started singing to the stars. "She's had her sex for the night." He was pretty cute, but the police who walked up on us didn't find him nearly as entertaining. They sent me back to my sister at the motel.

I left college in 1967 when my parents moved from Florida to Georgia. I wanted to work. Turned out it was the right thing for me. I started my 36 year career with the federal government at that small office in Albany, Georgia. When they called to set up the job interview I was in New York City visiting family. My mother gave them my resume over the phone. "She's a very nice girl." The job was waiting for me when I got home.

Socially it was the kiss of death. South Georgia, the Mecca of, let's see, *nothing*. Slim pickens in the dating arena. My first date was a guy I met at work. A nice looking, big old country boy. He had a few mannerisms that were a little jarring.

"Hey, how's it going?" He'd ask while at the same time his hand would be adjusting his crouch. It wasn't a sex thing, just his thing. I noticed he did it to the folks at work too. I wonder what he was hiding down there that constantly needed to be rearranged?

My parents lived in fear we would have sex and I'd get pregnant. Then country boy would be the family Bubba. My mother screened me carefully when we were going out.

"Just the movies, mom," I'd reassure her. "Don't worry so much."

I lied. That night we were heading to his place. I was thinking maybe I should check out his package myself, help him move it about a bit. Brave thoughts from a girl who had never seen what lies below.

Are mothers born with radars? I waved goodbye as I headed out and jumped in his car. His apartment was just a few blocks from the house. I rested my head on his shoulder and wondered just how far I might go.

Well I didn't get far at all. In fact, not even to the front door. While we were driving in one direction, my mom sent out a team to intervene in the other direction. We pulled into his drive to be greeted with my tiny elderly grandmother, still spry enough she walked several miles a day, and my kid brother.

Gotcha!

I walked back home with them and was actually relieved I was saved from myself. I was just nineteen and very naïve at that. He was almost thirty. That night ended any dating future but I still kept an eye on his hand maneuvers at work.

The hang out spot for those my age was Shoney's Big Boy restaurant. Family style food inside and drive in service outside. Best strawberry pie you could put in your mouth. One balmy South Georgia day I drove in for a burger with the girls and came out with a marine on my arm. He was stocky, good looking and had a nice smile. He was stationed at the base in town and was as bored as I was.

We dated briefly and then got married. I was a virgin and marriage was my answer to shed that title. The ceremony was small and informal. I wore a lavender suit that I sewed myself and a pillbox hat. The perfect little wife.

Only I was not so perfect. While dancing on our honeymoon I was eyeing the couple next to us thinking, *I'd rather be with that guy.* See what happens when you marry just to have sex rather than to marry because the sex is great?

It wasn't a bad marriage; it just was a marriage that was not meant to last. Good fortune had it that he fell in love with one of my friends from work and took off with her. Now I was free to find my true love.

I had ten years of dating after our divorce before I finally found Mr. Right. Dating during a period when sex was considered safe. My only thought was not to get pregnant. I never used a condom but was on the pill.

Did you know at that time you could also take the interest on your credit cards as a deduction on your federal taxes? *Now those were the good old days.* It paid to be a shopaholic back then.

Finally in my mid thirties I met the man who would become my life long mate. First kiss told me so. Thank goodness I didn't have to wait until I got married to have sex. That pressure off, it did take us forever to get married.

I was on birth control pills right until I went through menopause. Never missed a beat at sex, and never missed a period. How easy was that? I went from playing the field to settling down with the man I loved.

Now at age sixty I get to do it all over again. Sex. Not ready, not anxious, but something to reckon with I am sure.

I call my husband's cousin back. "So this silver bullet thing, have you got one?"

Decorating and Widows

"Well now you can decorate the way you want." What idiot said that to me? Oops! My best friend.

She knew that my husband and I never agreed on how the house should look and between the two of us we kept it a mess.

"You always find the best stuff." She was eyeing some things I purchased at the antique show earlier that day. "Where are you going to put those?"

I looked at vintage rose oil painting and the small painted washstand I'd just hauled into the kitchen and shrugged. "Don't know." Then I laughed. "Do I ever?"

I was a collector turned antique dealer. Bad enough I had *my* things everywhere, but I had corners and tabletops piled high with *stuff* to price and sell. While I rented a storage unit for the overflow, many times between shows furniture would sit in the house waiting to be reloaded in the van.

"I see she's layering furniture now," a friend of my husband's said after I came back from a buying trip. A sideboard, bed and dresser were lined up in the sunroom, one in front of the other.

I deal in vintage art and my husband wanted posters from Ikea.

He built modern furniture as a hobby. "These hinges are Swedish and will last a lifetime."

I'd give him my snappy reply, dramatically thrusting my arm towards an old primitive cupboard. "Well this piece has lasted several lifetimes."

After he painted the living room walls I waited too long to pick which paintings to hang over the sofa. He decided he liked the white wall over the sofa best. That wall remained blank for ten years.

This drove me crazy. I'd try to barter with him. "Don't worry about a birthday present this year, hon. I'll just hang something over the couch." Didn't get anywhere with that one and didn't get to hang any paintings in the living room either. I made up for it in all the other rooms.

I had a great following at the Lakewood Antique Show for its last three years. Sadly the show ended in October 2006, breaking many antique dealers' hearts.

My customers loved my romantic cottage look; old painted furniture, Victorian floral paintings, vintage hooked rugs and 1940's barkcloth roses fabric panels. A look I loved too, but most men, especially my husband, didn't care for.

"I'll bet your house is lovely." A comment I heard many times during a show. "So your husband lets you decorate like this?"

I laughed to myself on that one and just thanked them for stopping by.

It was always like this with us. His mother brought him up on walnut and mahogany, fine pieces of furniture with marble tops, pristine finishes, burled wood and inlays. He loved to build cabinets with birch. And his favorite style was Danish Modern.

I am just the opposite. I love old pieces that show their age and have painted finishes. If a table was a little rickety it only charmed me more. The more distressed a piece of furniture, the better it looked to me.

Perhaps my husband's secret gift to me was his *no* on all the changes I thought we needed over the years. If I had decorated the house the way I wanted, I would have had nothing to do when he died. With my small antique space I could spend my days switching things out from the house to my booth and my nights rearranging what I had purchased.

Some of the dealers would quiz me on what I brought to the shop. We all like to know where to buy the best stuff.

"Where did you get that piece?" A dealer liked the modern chest of drawers I was putting in my booth. Then she winked and smiled, "I know, your husband's. Same as with that inlay table, huh?" It was sad and fun all at the same time. Every piece that left was solid and modern; everything that came in had to be knocked with a hammer to tighten its joints.

My house was full of life when my husband was alive, but it was a mess to look at. His presence filled every inch of space. His deep voice resonated down the halls. Three thousand square feet hardly seemed big enough for us. Now there are rooms I rarely see.

All my older friends talk about downsizing. I downsized too. My 6' 7" husband is gone. My house, our old house, is just as I had envisioned it would be if I could decorate it with abandon. While lovely to look at now, it is missing the one touch that no decorator can supply, the love of a husband that made the house a home at the end of the day.

Menu For Home Alone Pity Party.

It's fun to create your own and makes a crap day special.
Stuffing your face with sinful delights may be just the
tonic for what ailes you.

Dress: Long T-shirt, Bunny Slippers
No RSVP, It's Only Me Again
Large Bag Of Potato Chips,
Shit, Make That Two
Onion Dip
Fudge Brownies
Slice Of Leftover Pizza
Bottle of Sherry
Diet Coke
A Generous Heapin Of Pity Pie,
Or Maybe, Coconut Pie. Yum.
Dog Bones
(The Dogs Only Like Me When I Feed Them)
Turn off cell, no one ever calls
Kleenex
Chick Flicks

Summer

I'd Rather Be At The Beach

The Man Of My Dreams

A story with a romantic twist, a plot full of intrigue, a handsome leading man and two girls scheming to find the perfect mate. That's how I would describe the actions leading up to meeting my future husband. A romp as fun as any book you'd like to read at the beach.

"You know, you never really took me out." I always gave my husband a hard time on that one. "I don't think we've ever had a real date."

He would always laugh and tease me. "You took me from that other girl. I didn't have to date you. You were pretty easy."

It's true. I switched dates with my girlfriend and found the man of my dreams. We each had a date that weekend, but with the wrong guy. The solution made sense to us, we would swap guys.

That was back in 1984 when dating seemed so simple. You met men in real life, at bars, at parties, through friends and work. I was in my mid thirties. There was no Internet dating service, no online chat rooms, no instant messaging. Makes you wonder how people ever got together without today's technology.

That same year I became friends with a heavy set Jewish guy from New York, who couldn't get a date in Atlanta to save his life. He rented an office and started a video dating service. I don't know if his plan was to make money or finally get laid. But he went ahead with his idea and became a small success. For a moderate fee you would visit his office, answer a list of questions and talk about yourself. He taped the interview and then would share it with others who had joined his dating club.

"Come on, help me here, make a video," he called me one sunny afternoon. "I need a guinea pig to get this project started." He had already signed up men, but he was short on females.

"No, thanks." I liked the bars. Even if I didn't meet a man, I got free food at happy hour. Video spelled porn to me.

"Buy you lunch and it's free to join."

"Lunch, huh." Food always appealed to me. "Where? No sleazy burgers."

He picked a spot that sounded fun and I agreed to make a dating video.

"Video first, then lunch." He was pretty bossy. "And wear something solid in color so it won't distract from your silly face."

That made me chuckle. "Yeah, that silly face you tried to kiss once." But we became good friends after that.

It was fun. I felt like a TV anchor. I talked into the camera and answered a series of questions. My video was completed in less than an hour. He had a small gallery of videos of guys. So I took a look. A handsome chiseled face got my attention.

"Who is that?"

"He's new in town. Moved here from Spain about six months ago to start his business."

"Show him my video." Maybe this would work.

We did meet for dinner. He was just like his video, but too foreign for me. I like good old American jocks. The date was fun, but I didn't want to see him again.

The next day my friend called to tell me about her date the previous night. "Bored me to tears. All he talked about was backpacking and camping. My ex loved all that crap too. You know me, city gal."

I agreed with her. I am a city girl too.

"I need to introduce you two," she took me by surprise.

"Why? Doesn't sound like we'd have anything in common."

"Well, he sure is good looking and he's a real estate broker. Aren't you looking for someplace to put your license?"

She was right. While I worked for the feds my entire life I had a lot of part-time ventures over those same years. Getting my real estate license was just one.

"Point taken. And come to think of it, you would love my guy from last night." So we plotted on how to make this work.

I think both she and I missed our true calling in life. We should have worked for the State Department. The diplomacy with which we exchanged men was quite amazing. No one felt rejected, but the male ego being what it is, the two men met at a party a few weeks later and did not like each other. But the swap turned out to be kismet.

I went for a job interview with the realtor. We met at his office, a 1920's storefront he had renovated in a trendy neighborhood, Virginia Highlands. At five I entered his office and by midnight I was sitting on his lap kissing him. I placed my license with him the following week, but he called me the next night to get together.

"I'll be at a friend's house Friday night trying out his hot tub. He's out of town for the weekend. Come join me."

I didn't need to think twice. "Sounds great, give me the directions," I tried not to purr. I drove to meet him after work on Friday. The night was warm, the water warmer as I snuggled down beside him in the hot tub. He turned and kissed me and as they say, the rest is history.

A Dog Named Boy

Who would have guessed a dog would close the deal for me with the realtor? Proof positive that dogs are man's best friend.

We were enjoying a restful Saturday afternoon at the house. I decided to make a quick run down the street to the grocery store for more beer and something for dinner.

"Won't be long," I bent over for a quick kiss. "What should I pick up?"

"Surprise me." He was enjoying his cold beer and couldn't have cared less about anything at that moment.

As soon as I pulled up in the parking lot my attention was directed to an old man and his dog sitting in front of the liquor store. I bypassed the grocery store and headed straight over to them. Can't resist petting every dog I see.

"Lady, please take my dog," his arm was resting protectively over the pup. "I can't keep him and he needs a home." The man's breath reeked of wine. I looked at the dog nibbling on an open bag of Cheetos. He was black and tan and looked to weigh about forty pounds. Still young, he had not grown to fit the size of his paws.

I ruffled the pup's fur and could feel the grime caked in his thick undercoat. He looked up at me with wolf colored eyes and my heart melted.

I wonder....

"I'll be right back. There's someone who needs to see this dog." With that I got into my car and headed back in the direction I just came from.

"Guess what I found?" Even before he could answer I rattled on about the pup. "Come look at him, please." I was pulling on his hand to get him off the couch.

"OK, let's go. But you need to drive, too many beers." And that may have been the turning point on how we got a dog. *Too many beers.*

As soon as we pulled up my husband looked out the window and shook his head. "Part German Shepherd. Did I ever tell you I was bit by one as a kid?" But he opened the door and went towards the pair. I watched as he kneeled down, his tall frame still towering over the dog and wino, and gently ran his hands over the pup. To my amazement he picked up the pup, handed the man some bills, and got back in the car. The last thing I saw as I backed out of the lot was the man heading into the liquor store.

"This dog stinks." A foul odor permeated the car as soon as we shut the doors. We rolled down the windows to be able to breathe. "I'm giving him a bath as soon as we get home." I was pleased my husband was already claiming the dog as his.

So that is how we got Boy. The dog that played cupid to us as a couple. I was there most every night, but now I was needed to help with the dog. My responsibilities and possibilities were growing by the minute.

Boy was a wild ass puppy. He could race through the living room, jump on the couch, hit the wall and land standing on all fours. But at night he would lay quietly across my husband's long legs. The two became inseparable.

My husband gave his heart to that dog. I used to say to my girlfriends, "If it's me or the dog, I'm worried."

Boy grew up to be a magnificent dog. He topped out at ninety pounds, with a lot of his weight on his broad chest. His fur was long, black and silky with a thick undercoat. His bushy tail curled upwards. He was a mixed breed, but reminded us of one of the dogs we had seen in photos of the Iditarod one year. Not a husky, not a malamute, but some mixture in between. Powerful. Just like my husband.

The vet guessed Boy was four months old when we got him. We had him for twelve years before he got sick.

Boy had been to the vet on Friday for blood work. Later that night he vomited up everything he'd eaten in the past few days. I saw parts of Wednesday's meal from our dinner party.

"Boy needs to go to the emergency clinic," I told my husband first thing Saturday morning. I didn't want to wait for our regular vet on Monday.

We sat in the waiting room. I was getting impatient wondering what was taking so long. Boy had perked up on the drive over so he didn't look sick when we walked in.

Finally I couldn't stand it any longer. I walked up to the front desk. "Why haven't we been called yet?"

"You're next," she was apologetic. "We have a kid in here with his pet hamster. They are giving it CPR."

Please excuse my insensitivity here, but why would anyone give CPR to a hamster? Especially when there is a dog to be seen. Side note, the hamster did not make it and I felt badly watching the little boy cry.

Boy finally puked all over the waiting room floor, a wretched odor that was so vile they turned their attention to us and scurried us away to a back room. We had to leave Boy for tests. He had an IV for fluids and medicine. I left knowing this would not be good. But I couldn't voice my fear to my husband who was walking numbly to the car.

Sunday night my best friend came over to dinner. Halfway through the meal the phone rang. I answered it and my heart sunk.

"It's the clinic. Boy died." I could barely whisper this news to my husband.

My best friend came over to me and took the phone from my hand to hang it up. She understood.

My husband never said a word but went downstairs to his wood-shop. He did not come back up until he had built a casket for Boy.

I was the one who went to pick up Boy's body at 6AM from the clinic. My husband could not deal with it. But being the guy he was, he sent me out with the casket, screws and a screw gun to tighten the lid down after Boy was put inside.

Boy's body was completely wrapped in a white cloth when they brought him out to my car. He looked smaller than I thought his body should. I almost questioned them on that. But then I thought *who knows how they have to bundle bodies?* I left well enough alone and drove home.

We buried Boy in the back yard. It was a grey overcast nasty November day and the dirt turned to clay that turned to mud as the grave was dug deeper. My husband's casket was huge for the dog that was larger than life to him. We had to pull the casket out three times so my husband could dig the grave deeper and wider. By the time we got Boy underground I was thankful my husband hadn't dropped dead from dealing with the strain of it all.

Eleven bags of cement later a huge marker had been poured over Boy's grave. I grabbed a thin branch and wrote on the damp slab *We Love You, Boy.* The work was done.

A week later the phone rang and my husband answered it. He looked at me strangely and handed the phone to me. "It's the emergency clinic. They want to know when we are picking up Boy's body."

"I picked him up last Monday." I almost yelled at the guy on the other end. "Did I get the right body?" I remembered how I thought the package looked so small for Boy. *Why didn't I ask then?* I was left on hold for a minute.

"Sorry. You got him. They just forgot to take down the sign." The young voice at the other end apologized for the call and that was that.

Well, yes, I hope so I thought. I had not voiced my concerns to my husband the day I picked up Boy. He was upset enough. Now Boy was under eleven bags of cement and there was no way to check to see if the clinic was right or just covering its ass.

Boy's ass was already covered.

For some reason this struck us as funny, black humor on a day so dark. That ill placed call a blessing in disguise. From that day on when we talked about Boy we would laugh and refer to his gravesite as *The Tomb Of The Unknown Dog.*

The Family Tree

My *husband* was an only child. When he joined our family, small as it was, it was large on life. "Wait until you meet my folks," I bragged.

I had met his folks already and in the most embarrassing way. I had spent the night at his house and was trying to get dressed and out before his parents arrived later that day. They showed up early morning and caught me freshly out of bed.

They were pretty cool with it, thinking I was just another passing girlfriend. I knew I was going to be around and had hoped for a more dignified introduction. They found out soon enough they would be seeing lots more of me. Well, perhaps I should say seeing more of me. There isn't *lots more* to be seen when you are caught in your undies.

My husband met my parents a few weeks later. The family he had heard so much about coming to life in front of his eyes. I loved to tell him stories of my childhood.

"So you're from the Islands?" A remark I always got from strangers when I told them I was born in Jamaica.

"No, Jamaica, New York." How boring did that sound? Not even Manhattan, but *Queens*.

We moved from Jamaica to Long Island when I was still very young. I remember the newly built house and a muddy back yard that I ran for my life through, my mother not far behind trying to catch me.

"Better get down to June's," a phone call came in to my mother from a neighbor. "Looks like your daughter has taken off her underpants and is laying on the ground lifting her skirt up." What was I, six? Playing doctor with a boy of eight. A few kids watching. See, already sex on my mind and I didn't even know it.

I saw my mother racing towards us. I jumped up pulling my panties back under my skirt and ran towards home, passing her on the other side of the street. But she turned mid stride and chased me through the muddy back yard of our newly built house till she caught me. I was sent to my room. "I am very mad at you. You stay there until I tell you to come out."

Well within ten minutes she opened the door and my punishment was over. She gave me a hug, a coloring book and a lecture. "Don't do that again. You don't take your pants off. That can get you in trouble."

I guess I took her words to heart. At age 60 I still sleep with my knickers on and have been know to have sex with one leg still in my panties in case I need to escape quickly.

When I was nine we moved to Winter Haven, Florida. My dad and grandfather went into an automobile dealership together and headed south. Remember the Edsel? That was the year it was introduced. Lucky they also sold Lincoln and Mercury so when Edsel tanked they stayed afloat.

My dad was smart. He passed the New York bar exam first try. He had all his pilot ratings and flew small aircraft for fun. He wound up owning a car dealership with my grandfather because he was crazy for my mom.

When my grandfather died the business was sold and my dad finally got to do what he loved best. He went to work for a company in Albany, Georgia, that sold crop dusters, handling their legal work and taking on some charter flights. My dad died in 1989 at age 69 doing all the things he loved.

My mother stayed home with us as we were growing up. She was an action mother if you were bad. If you stuck out your tongue, you could end up tasting soap. If you threatened to run away, she'd pack your bag. We learned quickly how to behave, but we also learned she would back us on everything.

She inspired me by showing me you could be whatever you wanted at any age. She was a photographer and a writer, a creator of beautiful images.

She was sixty-one when my father died. She sold the house, moved to Florida, started her own business with art rubber stamps, traveled and took on the world of dating. She may have been the first cougar. I remember standing in the kitchen with my husband telling him, "Well, mom's thinking about marrying a guy a year older than you."

My husband looked at me in amazement. "Is she getting more sex than I am?"

We don't need to answer that one. But she decided not to marry the guy. He was too set in his ways for her.

My love of animals comes from my childhood and my mother's never ending interest in all critters. There were always new pets brought home, much to my dad's dismay. But after his initial *no* they all stayed.

My favorite pet was the Capuchin monkey, Baby, I got when I was 18. Also referred to as the organ grinder monkey. This monkey is usually pictured with street musicians in a little hat holding a tip cup. He filled most evenings with lively entertainment.

The pilots my dad worked with loved to come to our house for dinner. Between my mother's burgundy pot roast and Baby's antics there was never a dull moment. The men loved having this little monkey sit on their laps and reach his skinny fingers out to play with their jewelry. Baby would grab a ring or tie tack, roll his eyes and then try to put it in his mouth. A few fingers were gently nibbled.

"What is that in his hands?" A question we got a lot. Baby loved to sit in his cage and amuse himself for hours holding his plunger shaped penis. Try explaining that one and keeping a straight face. I found out later in life that this is not an unusual gesture for many of the male species.

Baby got wilder as he got older since we could not spend as much time with him. The Albany Zoo offered him a good home. We would go and visit him but he was too busy with his girlfriend to pay any attention to us. That plunger no doubt appreciated more there than at our house.

My mother has a special love of exotic animals. You never knew what would greet you on a visit to see her in St. Augustine. There was a huge Iguana caged on her balcony, a pet rat that could jump several feet from the ottoman to her lap, and an assortment of birds making it sound like the rain forest. Her talking parrot had a limited vocabulary, but he impressed the workman who was adding insulation to the attic with his one continuous question, "What ya doing?" It was embarrassing to hear the man trying to explain.

It was not unusual to be talking to Mother and have a little love-bird pop out of her cleavage. "Oh, forgot he was there," was all she would say. He liked to snuggle on her chest.

Today her household is calmer, with just a turtle and a cat.

My sister is a year younger than me. She is an artist, photographer and the great adventurer. She lived on a thirty-five foot sailboat cruising the Virgin Islands and surrounding areas for several years. She gathered rainwater with a bowl and cleaned her clothes beating them with rocks. After the boat life ended, she lived in a cottage over looking the bay in St. John, US Virgin Islands. She photographed Island life for commercial jobs. Now married to a Leprechaun, she is living in Florida. They are renovating their little shanty on the creek. She has a son and a granddaughter and still does art photography.

My brother is four years younger and lives in New York City. He grew up fascinated with old church pipe organs and is a classical musician. He is a church music director and owns an organ dealership. He is a performer and a businessman. His wife is involved in his music world and that was the bond that brought them together many years ago.

My brother is the family historian. My sister the official weeper. I am the worrier. All our bases were covered.

My dad and husband were friends sharing their interest of all things manly. I felt a connection with my dad long after his death because my husband and I could talk about him.

My brother and my husband disagreed on computers. You know that old Mac vs. PC thing. It got hot some times. But they laughed about it at my sister's Irish wedding a few years back and I am happy a friendship was found however briefly.

My mom and sis were just like me. We were silly girls around my husband. Annoyed when he tried to tell us what to do, smitten when he was just a big handsome guy to hug.

So many memories from childhood to widowhood of all the love a family can bring.

The Blue Cupboard

Some women have fantasies about sex. I had a fantasy about owning a blue cupboard. It is an odd fantasy I am the first to admit. I used to dream about this cupboard, primitive, large and with just a hint of old robins egg blue paint. I purchased several over the years and sold them. But I never brought one home. I don't know when this fantasy started, but I do know when it stopped.

The decorating magazines always tell you, *buy what you love, you'll find a place for it.* I took that advice to heart. I did find a place for all those things I loved, a storage unit that I had to pay rent on every month. My buying *what I loved* turned me into an antique dealer. An antique dealer who wanted to keep more than she sold.

The first blue cupboard I actually paid for but it never left the shop where I purchased it. A huge old European piece with doors that had beveled glass that sparkled in the light. It was the perfect color blue. I wrote a check immediately.

"I'll be back soon to pick it up." I waved as I walked out the front door. I was a frequent buyer there and they knew me well. I loved the size and color of that piece and thought *maybe I'll keep it.*

It was a month before I went back for the cupboard. It seemed to have grown in size with the reality I had to move it. *How was I going to get it in my car?* I did not own my van then, only a small station wagon. The piece was too large to squeeze into my small antique booth. I already had a storage unit so full something this size would not fit there either. And I had not yet started doing shows. I had no place to put my dream cupboard.

I looked at it in panic. The dealer I bought it from was working that day.

"Wish I'd never sold that piece." She gave me a strange look when she said that.

That look gave me a way out of my problem.

"Any chance you want to buy it back?"

I've bought back my own merchandise more than once, and so have other dealer friends of mine. Buying back our stuff is an illness to a small part of the trade.

She was thrilled. I left the shop relieved of my burden.

A few weeks later I was back shopping. The blue cupboard was still in her booth. On it a big sold sign, but I knew that just meant she had not had time to move it. The cupboard beckoned to me, teased me and darn if I wasn't sorry I'd given it up.

"Can I buy it back?" I begged her.

"No way," she shook her head. "It's going to the beach house in a few weeks."

I stood there looking at that old cupboard as though it were the man that got away.

The next blue cupboard that caught my eye appeared a few years later in a shop about an hour from the house. It was an 1800's step back cupboard, again huge in size, old blue paint with a creamy white interior. I thought it would be perfect in the sunroom, and of course, if it didn't fit, I could always sell it. A rationale I used for all my frivolous purchases. Priced way to high it would require a little bargaining and I wanted to ask if it could be delivered.

I phoned the dealer from home. "What's your best price?" Words dealers hate to hear but it is part of the business. We had just agreed on a price when I heard my husband yelling for me from the sunroom.

"Come quick. Something is wrong with Jake. He can't walk."
Jake our 95-pound German Shepherd. I went and looked at Jake
and knew he was in trouble. Minutes earlier he had been walking
past me in the living room and now he was unable to move his hind
legs. I cancelled the cupboard and focused on money for Jake's vet
bills. Money well spent because Jake did walk again within a few
months.

I still wondered why did a blue cupboard haunt me so? I thought
back to the first time one had captured my attention. It was early in
our relationship and I was at a favorite antique show alone, as I usually was. He was not a shopper.

It was a simple blue cupboard, more of a hutch with open shelves
at the top. It had a hold sign on it. I asked the dealer about it.

"Sweetest couple," he told me. "They are still shopping, finding
antiques for their new home." He grinned at me. "Husband didn't
really like it but his wife loved this one. Pretty sure they will buy
it."

I felt a bit of a pang when the dealer said that. Later I felt a little
envy at how the couple looked at each other as they paid for the
cupboard. They had showed up right as I was leaving. I wanted to
be the gal who had the man that said, "Yes honey, if that's what you
want, we'll get it."

Those words never came out of my husband. But I never asked
him if I could buy something. I was an antique dealer and bought
what I loved, sometimes to sell, sometimes to keep. We weren't
married then, but living together. The house was his house, but our
place to be together.

I wanted him to be the guy who would say, "Yes, if you love it."
My husband would have looked at that worn painted cupboard and
said, "It's a piece of crap."

The old blue cupboard was a symbol of what I thought was missing with us. It started my quest for that perfect cupboard to make my life complete. A quest that ended when I realized my life was complete. I had the perfect man for me.

In reality my husband was that old cupboard I dreamed about. He was huge in size. He was strong and solid. His foundation was built on principles and family values. He passed the test of any good antique, how it weathers time and only gets better with age. He mellowed well. Just like the old wood cupboard we had our small rough patches but our structure was sound. Over the years the patina of our relationship was as warm and inviting as any primitive cupboard that had a lifetime behind it.

I no longer dreamed about a blue cupboard and put that fantasy to rest. I was still buying things during the day that horrified my husband. But at night when we went to bed my dreams and fantasies were only of those he and I could enjoy together.

The Male Who Rules My Life

He lifts his head up ever so slightly to look at me. Still damp from being bathed he is lying on a towel. My hands are moving over his body, lifting his leg slightly. He is curious as I reach for my hair-dryer. "It's OK," I whisper. Satisfied his head drops back down and he waits for my next move.

Almost sounds like a porn scene. But I am grooming my male dog Jake. He has no use of his back legs and he is incontinent. I have to bathe him regularly. He weighs 95 pounds.

My vet suggested the hair dryer. "The dry heat may keep infections away if he'll let you use it."

I look at that big bear of a dog. My how he loves to be pampered. He has ruled my life for twelve years.

It was Labor Day weekend all those years ago when I first set eyes on Jake. There was a commotion in the front yard that became loud enough to get our attention in the house. The neighbors were trying to catch two stray dogs, a German Shepherd and a black poodle mix.

"Come on." I tugged at my husband's arm as I headed for the door. "Let's see if we can help."

The shepherd was circling the street in panic, the poodle had already made friends. After what seemed like an eternity both dogs were secured in my neighbor's fenced yard. Neither had tags and both dogs looked like they had been on the road for some time.

"Are those fish hooks in the poodle's fur?" I couldn't believe it, but there were small hooks embedded in the dog's curls. The shepherd had a badly mangled back leg and walked with an odd limp.

"Let's place an ad in the paper to see if anyone claims them." My neighbor was worried someone was missing a pet. I knew no one would call. The dogs had most likely been dumped.

We got both dogs to the vets the next day. The German Shepherd had heartworms, an infection and that bad back leg. The pad on his back paw was sheered off. He was horribly underweight at 65 pounds. Most likely he would not have lasted much longer on the streets.

I knew he was our dog from the moment I saw him. I named him Jake.

For those dog lovers like myself who are now asking, "What about the poodle mix?" He is living happily with my neighbor.

"You should have named him Houdini," my vet told me when I called to see how Jake's heartworm treatment went. Not so good. Jake had broken out of his cage and went on a rampage through the clinic the previous night.

I was afraid to ask, but did. "Is he OK? How much damage did he do?"

"Jake is fine," my vet was laughing. "He broke that latch, pulled a metal kick plate off the back door and ate a lot of cat food."

They came in to find him sitting quietly in his cage.

"So, does this mean I can't board Jake there?" I was teasing my vet and he knew it. I never board my dogs.

"Not without a thousand dollar deposit," his quick reply.

I had to take Jake home that day. But Jake had many years of visits to see our favorite vet man.

Having a male dog with so many health problems made me ask the silliest of questions. I was either calling or taking Jake in to be checked.

My latest question may have topped all others.

"Max, Jake's butt hole looks like it's getting darker." That is what happens when you watch a dog run the yard with his tail up in the air and you are an idiot.

My vet looked at me with the straightest of faces and replied, "Barbara, butt holes are people we don't like. That is his anus." Then we both cracked up over that one. Jake was fine. I was the one with the problem.

Almost normal would describe Jake as he aged. Those first few years with him were hum dingers. Our vet guessed Jake was four years old when we got him. A gentle, sweet big dog with a very timid personality. Everything frightened him.

"He was probably mistreated and it has done some damage."

The vet didn't tell me anything I didn't know.

We couldn't leave Jake alone without coming home to paintings knocked off walls and chairs tossed like toys. He had severe separation anxiety.

Jake outdid himself eating my 1800's cottage painted washstand. I walked in the kitchen after work and noticed that it was pushed away from the window. I went to ask my husband why he moved it.

"I didn't touch it." He was now as curious as I was.

We went to look at it . The entire back corner had been eaten. Jake had a panic attack of some sort. Not even a wood chip on the floor.

"You're on poop patrol now." My vet told me to keep an eye on Jake. I stuffed him with bread so there was something in his stomach besides antique pine.

Two months after my husband died Jake's back legs started to loose their strength. Within another month he could not stand.

"OK, Jake, up!" I lifted Jake with a sling under his hind end and he could walk on his front paws. Sometimes I'd give him a ride in the wheelbarrow. He loved that.

Jake soon became inconterient. I found a belly band online that held Kotex pads to control the problem. Jake didn't mind wearing it. He was still a happy boy.

Four years earlier Jake had the same problem with his legs. Nothing showed up on his tests. I didn't take him for surgery because he would not have handled it. I just wanted to keep him comfortable.

"Why not try acupuncture?" my vet suggested. "May help relax those back legs." He suggested I contact Loving Touch Animal Center in Stone Mountain, Georgia. I did.

"Such a handsome boy," the pretty vet would tell Jake when he came for his treatments. He loved his acupuncture sessions and getting his Qi in order. We would sit on the floor and it was our quiet time together. One needle was placed gently in the top of his head, the calming zone, the rest ran down his back and onto his legs. Some of those needles had wires clipped to them that went to a battery pack. Thirty minutes later we were ready to go. We did this every week. Within a few months Jake was walking again. A miracle I had not expected.

During those months I moved to the living room to keep an eye on Jake at night. I'd start bedtime with my husband then I'd slip out to sleep on the couch to be with the dogs the rest of the night.

"You have the best of both worlds," I told my husband. "Sex and then I am gone. Kind of like a great date." I am not sure he saw it quite in those terms.

My husband asked me once, "When are you coming back to bed?"

"Outlive the dog," I playfully answered him.

That remark still haunts me. My husband did not outlive the dog. My husband was not sick when I said that and we had no clue what was to come later with his health. Jake was our concern at that time. I had the night watch and my husband had the day watch.

After Jake started walking again I still spent many nights on the couch. I liked to watch movies at the midnight hour.

When my husband became ill my sleeping with the dogs became a topic of humor.

"How is your husband's breathing at night?" the lung doctor asked me.

My husband laughed and answered for me. "She wouldn't know, she sleeps with Jake."

The doctor looked at us in confusion. "Who's Jake?"

So even then I sounded *unfaithful*, sleeping with another male. The doctor chuckled when we told him it was the handicapped dog.

In the last months I have held Jake's face in my hands telling him, "If you're tired buddy and need to go, I'll be OK." But then I give him my promise. "I'll take care of you as long as you want."

I made that same promise to my husband. But my husband hated illness and left me before the worst hit him.

Jake, on the other hand, has adjusted to his limitations. He shakes his thick mane and the dog who rules my life is not ready to say "goodbye".

On Buying Poise Ultra Pads At Age Sixty

It's late Friday night when I realized I forgot to buy pads for Jake's belly band. With a dog that size you can't wait until the next day to shop or heaven help you there will be a lake of pee across the floor.

I called my best friend as I tried to get the energy to head out.

"Doesn't this just suck?" I asked her. "It's 10PM on a Friday night and I have to go out to buy Kotex for the dog."

She laughed and so did I. How symbolic was this of my dating life and how I spent my weekends.

I marched into Kroger and went straight to the counter marked *incontinence* and grabbed the largest box of the pads I could find. Not Kotex, but Poise Ultra Pads with extra thickness. Why the hell they have to package these things in Pepto Pink wrappers is beyond me. You can't sneak those past anyone in the checkout line.

I picked up a few other small items since I was at the store. The pads were at the back of my purchases in the checkout line. Somehow the Indian girl at the register missed them when she rang up my other items.

I reached back to grab the edge of the box for her. "You forgot these," I told her. Then feeling somewhat embarrassed since I *was* 60 and she might think they were for me I felt compelled to say, "Oh, these are for my dog."

Well she had no idea what I said but the three young guys the next aisle over looked around to see what I was talking about. And there, big as life, was the huge pink box of Poise Ultra pads.

Oh crap. I just knew they thought the pads were for me.

My face turned red and in my mind I could hear them saying, *Right, lady, they're for your dog.*

As I wheeled my cart out the door I thought about that scene. Maybe the pads should have been for me. I started laughing so hard I almost peed in my jeans.

The Bracelet And
The Electrician

I had a husband who could repair everything. He could build anything. He moved houses early in his career as a realtor. We never called a plumber or an electrician. His joy was in having a list of repairs and getting to work on them. Me? I can't do diddlysquat.

I loved the older houses in the downtown area of Atlanta and owned a 1940's brick bungalow I bought in the early 1980's before I met my husband. I had no idea the work it took to own a house. I just knew I wanted to decorate. As I look back on that house I am amazed I survived it.

My old apartment had an electric stove, as did the other apartments before it. My house had a gas stove, an alien appliance to me. The knobs to turn on the burners were gone but the knob for the oven was still there. I don't usually cook, but I invited a good friend of mine over for dinner my first week in the house. I figured I could bake something.

"Shouldn't take long to warm this." I smiled at my friend and my casserole. It looked quite yummy. I turned the only knob on the stove and heard a loud *whoosh*, a sound I was not familiar with from my days of electric stoves. She had about as much experience with gas stoves as I did. We looked at each other nervously.

"Let's eat out," I suggested to her. "My treat." I reached over and turned the oven off. We made a dash for the door.

The next morning I called a repairman. He came quickly and looked at my stove while handing me a bag of knobs.

"Works fine, lady." He had turned the oven on and off.

"Can you do something since this is costing me $25 for your visit?" I felt quite silly I had called him.

He reached out, grabbed the bag of knobs back and put them on for me. Then he smiled crumpling the empty sack and tossed it in the trash can. I wrote him a check.

It was summer when I moved into my house. The kitchen was tiny and the room was too warm for comfort. I realized the heat from the stove was adding to the problem. I blew out all the pilot lights and stood there feeling quite proud of myself to have come up with such a simple answer to cool the kitchen.

I called my mother and boasted about what I had done.

"You blew out the pilot lights?" Her tone made me nervous. "Oh dear God," she was mumbling on the other end. Now I was really worried.

"Honey, you could blow up the house. Get a match and re-light those pilots." She stayed on the phone while I did this in case there was an explosion she would know. Better than hearing it on the evening news I suppose.

Right after I met my husband, in those few weeks before I started staying at his place, I noticed there was a gas odor in the basement around the furnace. I mentioned this to my neighbors, two lesbian gals who knew how to fix things.

"It's simple," the one gal told me. "Get a bucket of sudsy water and a rag. Hit each joint on the pipes leading to the furnace and when you find the leak, the soap will bubble up."

I called my future husband. "I've got to check on the furnace, find the leak. So I'll be late." Then I told him I was going to try the soapy water.

He was not privy to my earlier fiasco with the gas stove and did not realize I was an idiot on these things. "Hell, just light a match and check each joint." I did not hear him laughing at his own joke as he hung up.

His suggestion sounded so much simpler and after all, he was the great renovator. I went into the basement with a box of wooden matches and I certainly did find that gas leak. The flame burst into the air as I hit the final joint, missing me by a hair thank goodness. I smiled, very pleased with myself and called him back.

"Your suggestion worked like magic!"

From that day on he did not give me advice on home repair but came to the house and took care of the problem himself.

Now I am living alone in a large rambling brick ranch house built in the 1950's. There is a small cottage outside and two other out buildings behind it. The yard is substantial. My husband took care of this house for nearly 22 years. His best friend advised me to sell. "You don't need that much space, and who will do the work?"

Well he is right, *who*? It is a big question. I can't even reach the outside lights to replace the bulbs. But the house is my home, was our home, and I have no plans to move.

My first repair problem came two months after my husband died. Summer was here with its hot humid air and I was running the window A/C units full tilt. That night I steamed rice for the dogs and when I pulled the steamer plug from the wall socket, both were very hot to my touch. I went back later and the wall socket was still warm. I looked at the A/C unit at the far end of the kitchen and figured something was definitely wrong with the electrical line running that wall.

"Call an electrician," one of the dealers at the antique shop said when I went in the next day complaining about the problem. "Hell, a fire could start in your walls."

That scared me into action.

I called an old buddy of my husband's. "I need an electrician. Do you know someone?"

He gave me a phone number and a name, Randy. I called and Randy was coming in the morning.

That night rummaging through my jewelry box for some things to take to the shop I found an old silver bracelet I had bought a few years back. The bracelet was sterling with two hearts monogrammed *Barbara Loves Randy*. After I bought it I told my husband I should have Randy removed and his name engraved on it. But I never did anything with it and tossed it back in a box of things marked *later*.

I looked at that bracelet and wondered, *Could Barbara Love Randy?* My bracelet says it's so. I spent the rest of the night in good humor enjoying my private joke.

The next morning Randy appeared on time at my house. Mid forties, tan, sandy hair, muscular arms, good looking, dressed in shorts and a T-shirt. A god had been sent to fix my electrical problem.

He found the problem easily and replaced a socket going bad. He stayed and played with my dogs and talked about moving here from California. The more he talked the more I felt comfortable chatting with him. He was playful and I decided to show him the bracelet. He did not have a wedding band and I couldn't resist the temptation to ask, "Are you single?"

He was endearing with his reply, he had a life partner, he was gay. "Yep, all the good ones are either married or gay," he laughed kindly as he said it.

Or dead, I thought. I just smiled at him and nodded my head in agreement.

After Randy left I looked at that bracelet, chuckled and tossed it in the box of things to go to the shop to sell. There would be no

Randy in my future. Unless, of course, god forbid, I had more electrical problems, so I thought twice about pitching his business card.

My husband was Mr. Fix-it. Sure he complained when he had to haul that big leather tool bucket of his on all our trips to see the family. But you couldn't have gotten him to leave it home if you tried. He took care of our house, he helped my girlfriends with their houses, he took care of his mother's house in North Carolina, and he worked on my mother's house in Florida. There was always a *honey do* list somewhere for him to tackle. He never left a thing undone.

Who would have expected he would leave me with the biggest repair of all? A broken heart that needed to be mended.

Looking For Mr. Good Date

What is that old saying? If you get a lemon, make lemonade. Lemons, that sums up most of my dating experiences since my husband's death. Lemons that were so tart you couldn't make anything out of them. Some of them even a little rotten.

I started dating way too soon after my husband died. But, gee, I had absolutely nothing to do, no job, no children, just the dogs and an antique booth that had a life of its own. I lunched with my girlfriends who had their husbands at home at night. I was gobbling up my best friend's life with my constant calls. The night, always my favorite time of day, was leaving me unnerved alone.

At 2AM, my favorite hour to be on the computer, I was crying, sobbing so hard my head was bobbing over the keyboard. I had my usual auction site up and when I glanced at it an ad popped up for an online dating service. A photo of a handsome guy smiled at me and the words *look for free* beckoned me to visit their site. I crumpled my Kleenex, tossed it in the trash and thought, *why the hell not?*

I clicked on the link and was quickly taken to my first online dating site. *Whoa,* this looked more interesting than the paintings I was eyeing only moments ago on Ebay. I quickly made up my user name and started enjoying the view. Oh my, men everywhere. All sizes, ages and colors. I pulled out my trusty credit card, the one that still had available money on it, and hit the *join now* button. Suddenly my lonely night had company.

My first venture in the online dating services was in August, three months after my husband's death. Too soon for dating, but not soon enough for me to have a little diversion from my tears. It was hard work for me, trying to make myself sound desirable when I felt like a fish out of water. The questions you have to answer to complete your profile confused me. I thought I knew myself, but I knew my old self. This new gal alone on her own had not yet had time to develop. *What are your interests? What are you looking for in a mate?* A harsh reality hit me. *I had no answers.* I didn't even have questions. What seemed so simple stymied me as a fresh widow.

I put on my thinking cap wanting to be sharp and witty. It turned out I picked up my dunce cap instead.

If you were a single guy, would this make you hot? *Looking for a friend only. I buy my clothes at thrift stores and have two dogs, one handicapped.*

I leaned back in my chair exhausted. But my profile was up there. I paid for one month's membership. I was positive that in 30 days I would find a cure for the blues.

Surprisingly enough I got some attention.

My first date was amusing. I use that word because I couldn't really take this seriously. Serious was having my husband die, dating was a folly to be taken lightly. I made up some dating rules to keep me safe. *Do not give out my home address,* rule number one. Secondly, *meet only in a public location*, one preferably that serves food.

I also e-mailed my best friend all the information on my date right before I headed out. In case I didn't reappear there was a starting point to look for my body.

All my bases were covered and I was ready.

The night of my first real date I was actually excited. I hadn't been out after dark in awhile and that was its own adventure. I played dress up in my vintage finds fresh from the thrift shop, but made sure I wore only the pieces with designer labels. I was decked in my usual heavy load of turquoise jewelry, Capri's and a white lace blouse.

"We'll meet at the Tapas bar closer to your side of town," my date suggested. While I don't give out my address, the site does give a general area. Mine was Decatur. "I live in Marietta, and that's too far for you to drive." How thoughtful. I was encouraged.

I walked into the restaurant and there he was, sitting at the bar just as he promised. He was the age he told me, early fifties, but where was that heavier hunk of a man in the photos? This man was reed thin, tall with thinning blonde hair. The photo showed me a man on a bike with some meat on him and thicker hair.

"Oh I see," I said later when he told me his photo was a few years old.

I proceeded to drink a Margarita to calm my nerves and got thoroughly drunk. I really don't drink, but like the idea of a cocktail when I am out. "Maybe a cup of coffee before we head on." I needed to get my grip back.

"I know a great place to go where there is music and we can talk," he eyed me drinking my coffee and I wondered what sort of gal he thought I was. Tipsy so soon.

The next place *was* nice. We sat at the bar.

"Just water for me," I smiled at a handsome young bartender. *Now why wasn't he my date?*

It was Tuesday night and the place was quiet. A young couple at the bar started talking to us. My date got involved talking politics with the husband and I had the best time with his wife. My date and I never spoke, except for the occasional hug he came back to place on my neck.

"I like your boyfriend," the girl smiled.

"On no, he's not my boyfriend. Just met him." From there we went on to talk about my husband and she listened with tears in her eyes. Wish I could have seen her again.

My date? He was at the other end of the bar drinking beer after beer with her husband until way after midnight.

I didn't care I liked talking to my new gal friend.

Then we began the death defying drive back to my car. I was sober. He was not. *Why did I think it was a good idea to go in his car?* I asked myself as I gripped the dash.

"Listen to this," he popped a CD in. "My favorite song." He started singing something I couldn't understand, his car swaying all over the road. Finally we got back to where I had parked earlier. *Thank you* I whispered to the man above.

Just as I reached for the door to hop out he grabbed for me. He planted a kiss on my lips and his hand grabbed my right breast over my blouse. He was more drunk than aggressive so I was not worried. I could have decked him in a second if needed. Extra pounds come in handy sometimes.

His moves were so reminiscent of my high school years I had to smile. *Do guys still do this I wondered?* He assured me he was *bad* in the bedroom (and to this day I am not sure if he was bragging or warning me he was no good). I jumped out of the car and laughed on my drive home. The night air was exhilarating, even if the date had been flat.

I e-mailed him the minute I got into the house. *Thanks for a lovely night, but I think you are looking for more than I am.*

The next day I got the reply every gal hopes for, *oh don't mind me, I am always like that when I am drunk.*

Not to be discouraged I looked at my next match. A photograph of man in his early sixties with thinning black hair greeted me. His hobby was building large model war bird planes and flying them at club meetings. He sounded nice in his profile, down to earth and friendly.

We developed an e-mail friendship and then the dreaded message came. *I think I am being captivated by you.* He was a nice man, but I was not looking to captivate anyone. I wrote back, *Please don't, I just want a friend.* So friends we became for a short while.

He owned a vintage Corvette he was trying to sell. I have no interest in cars, but on my 60th birthday a few weeks later, this car became a topic of conversation over a few beers. Two of my girl-friends decided to take me somewhere a little off my beaten path to celebrate my birthday. We ended up at a club that has the reputation of being a pick up spot for older folks. I cringed at the thought that I was sitting at a table at a place I had laughed about since arriving in Atlanta in my late twenties.

Of course no men approached us but we weren't very inviting.

"Did you see that beehive hairdo?" my one girlfriend giggled as she took a slug of beer from her almost empty bottle. "And that white lacy dress? I think I had one like that for my prom."

My other friend joined her in pointing out the obvious. "Polyester plaid pants, who wears those anymore?"

"This is not helping." I started to feel a panic attack coming on. The disco ball in the center of the dance floor made me dizzy as I watched couples my age dancing to old forties tunes.

My two friends with their secure relationships started poking gently at my arm. "Get out there, walk around the bar, bet you'll find someone to dance with." Oh, that was a creepy thought.

Instead I twirled my beer bottle and started talking about the Corvette. The car began to take on a life of its own and I got ex-cited. *Why not* I thought. *A hot car rather than a hot guy*, that is my answer. Of course, I am still not sure what was the question.

The first thing the next morning I called my friend. "Hold that car for me. I'm coming out Monday to buy it."

I am now the proud owner of a 1979 white Corvette Stingray. I did my homework over the weekend on prices and insurance before I went to buy it. Did I mention I am not a car person? Owned three cars in my entire life, each one was the only car I looked at and then bought. So it never dawned on me to look at other Corvettes. This was my car. It found me through the dating service. Not what I had planned on, but exactly what I needed.

When I drove out to buy the car I had a small panic attack. *Should I do this? Can I afford it?* My answer was if I didn't do this I would never take a wild chance on anything again. It was the right thing to do for my self-image, for my sense of adventure and while I rarely drive it, I smile every day I see it parked in my driveway. No muscular man that month, but a handsome muscle car of my very own that does chase away the blues.

So lets sum up month one of dating: Membership fee $59.95, Boyfriend zero, Corvette Stingray $10,000, experience priceless.

And to think this is just the beginning of dating and meeting men.

Fall

*Well, this day was a
total waste of makeup.*

Fall Sneaks In My Window

I rush down the long winding driveway to pick up the mail. God it is chilly. *When did that happen?* I am still running the A/C in the house, but the air outside is much cooler. Shit, another season with its new share of memories. I shudder and head back to the house. I am not ready for this.

My mailbox is still full of insurance notices and medical bills. *How can a human life end so quickly, yet paperwork has a never-ending life?* Those bills, a painful reminder that more than the season has changed. I feel nauseous.

I toss the mail on the counter and grab my bottle of sherry. I have found that a bit of sherry in my favorite old etched glass has a way of comforting me. I feel elegant sipping from the antique glass and it makes a pity party more festive. I fill my glass almost to the top. It will take the chill out and settle me down. I feel a slight burning sensation in my throat with the first sip, warming me as no sweater can.

Today has taken me by surprise. *When did summer pass?* Perhaps summer tucked its head down and left quietly, ashamed at what spring had done. And now fall is trying to sneak in my windows. "Go away," I whisper to the air around me, as though I can change the weather.

Fall is here. No doubt about it. Cool and brisk. I should open my windows, turn on the attic fan, allow the glory of fall enter my house. But I can't. I don't want to face another new season, another reminder my husband is gone. *I'll do it later, maybe.* I think it can wait for now.

I check my e-mails. I check them hourly. Boy do I need a life.

Please let there be a message, my mantra every time I hit the send and receive key.

A message comes in. *We may have something in common,* a new man has written me. *May Sarton. Your profile says you like her journals. I have them all.*

Wow. Someone who has read May Sarton. I thought I was alone on that one. Years ago I read all her books. Her journals of solitude on her life in Maine. Moving essays on the changes around her with each passing decade. I did not want that life, but there was a beauty in her words that touched me. Reading her books made me serene during those hectic years I worked. Now I am living that life of solitude alone in my house and it is not nearly as intriguing.

I e-mailed him back and hoped he was still on-line to reply. A new message came in within minutes.

Hey, let's meet for a quick bite to eat. His words tempted me. I was hungry and my house was smothering me with its stagnant air and closed windows. We decided to meet in downtown Decatur, minutes from my house and a quick drive from his place in Atlanta.

Be there in thirty. The pub on the square OK? He writes back.

I am relieved to have someone to meet. I hurry to change into my blue sweater and pull on my old boots. Not much time to fluff, but a quick dab of blush on my checks and a bit of gloss on my lips and I head out the door.

Sometimes I forget how much life there is in town at night. My husband and I rarely went out after dark. The pubs and cafes are overflowing with customers. Tables outside all the restaurants are full of friends talking and drinking. The small downtown area of Decatur was buzzing with activity. I started to feel relaxed seeing the night-lights and watching the flurry of activity of people walking the streets. *Yes, going out tonight is a blessing.*

Of course parking was a bitch. The little square around the court-house has limited spaces and I did not want to go further down the street to the parking deck. After circling the area for what seemed like ages a space freed up. One last fluff of my hair looking in the rear view mirror and I felt ready for anything.

As I jumped out of my van a man came out of the shadows laughing at me.

"Where did you learn to drive?" There was a gentle mocking tone to his voice. "I've been watching you try to park in this space for ten minutes."

He had a gentle face to match his voice. In his mid sixties he was about my height, very thin, dressed in jeans, a sweatshirt and a cap. Reminded me of an old hippy.

"Let's get a drink." He guided me to an empty table outside the pub. It was amazing we found a spot the place was packed. He had a glass of wine and I ordered black coffee. After all I had been drinking sherry. The night air was intoxicating by itself.

We got so wrapped up talking we forgot to order dinner. Sipping my hot coffee I listened while he told me about himself.

"Divorced, my wife left me for someone else. Have the kids at home with me at times, holidays and college breaks." He had his PhD and wanted to know where I went to school. I'm the gal who dropped out of college, so I left that question unanswered.

His hand reached out to hold mine as he talked. I pulled back automatically. I don't like strangers touching me. I am a hugger, I admit. When I meet someone or say goodbye I like a friendly hug. Holding hands was in a different category at this stage.

"Don't you like public displays of affection?" he questioned me, frowning slightly. This is a question they actually ask you in some of the dating questionnaires, *how do you feel about public displays of affection?* I felt I was living a dating survey. In my early days I had sex in cars, how is that for public display? But I am not telling him that. No good will come from that disclosure.

He reached for my hand again and I let him hold it for a brief minute before tucking it back in my jacket pocket.

"I do like holding hands," I told him, looking directly at eyes that were laughing at me. "But I am shy until I know you better." How many times have I said this? My new reply to men who grab. So prissy, but it works.

The sweet smell in the night air and the bustle of people relaxed me enough to spend some time talking to him. Our mutual love of May Sarton was all we had in common it turned out.

He bent forward towards my lips and I turned my head so his moist kiss landed on my cheek. *Damn. He is way too forward.* I playfully pushed at him, wanting to knock him off the stool. A gesture that might be fun if I dared.

It had gotten late and I needed to head home. "Thanks for a lovely evening." I was sincere. It was fun to be among the living.

He grabbed my hand and brought it to his lips with a flourish, "Maybe next time?"

I knew he would not call and I did not want to see him again. A cup of coffee on an early fall night was the length of this relationship.

Driving the two miles back to my house, my car windows wide open, the air making a mess of my short hair, I was singing to a favorite song on my radio. The stars were twinkling in the sky as though lighting my path home. *Damn it felt good to be out.*

As I pull into my driveway the dogs are howling from inside the house. A greeting that makes me smile. I unlock the side door. *I have been missed.* Foxy runs to greet me, jumping all over me as I enter the kitchen. Jake is laying on his mat in the dining room, howling, waiting for me to come to him.

"Hi, babies." I toss them a quick bone to tide them over until I can get to them. And I will, in a minute.

First I have to open the windows, turn on the attic fan. I twirl around in the glory of the breeze that encircles me. My fears vanish as the cool night air blows in with the fragrance of hope in a moonlit fall night. *Thank you,* I whisper to the man I will never see again. *Thank you for helping me let fall sneak in my windows.*

The Quickest Date Around

Coffee? The same message came in on my e-mail three times that week. Twice the week before. I went to the dating site and looked at his profile.

You will meet no one quite like me, his opening words boasted. I looked at his photo. Tall, reed thin, arms crossed he was leaning on a wall full of books. He looked like he was in his twenties. Soft languid eyes and long dark hair gave him a very feminine look. Something about his photo made me uneasy. *Don't think so.* I shuddered to myself as I popped the delete key. He definitely was not my type.

The next week the same e-mail message came in again, *coffee?*

What is it with this guy? I thought. *And why is no one else writing to me except this idiot saying 'coffee'?*

It was mid September and no matches had come in on my e-mails. I went back in and looked at his profile. He had added recent photos and looked surprisingly quite normal. Now I was looking at a man in his early fifties with short black hair, still thin but smiling pleasantly. He was not bad looking compared to his previous photo.

Since no one had shown much interest in me that week I thought *what the heck* and wrote him back, *coffee might be nice.*

He immediately e-mailed his phone number to me. He lived close by in Atlanta and suggested we meet at a coffeehouse in one of the local neighborhoods. *Call me* he added.

We spoke three times during a two-day period planning our meeting.

"Maybe we can go out on Saturday night too, *sweetheart*," he said, a very nice voice at the other end of the phone. He also called me *sweetheart* three times during our conversations.

I thought he acted as though we already had a relationship and I found that a bit odd. But then, dating is odd and I needed to get out of the house. I felt like the walls were closing in on me and a cup of coffee with a stranger might be a nice break from the silence surrounding me.

I looked in the mirror as I finished putting a little color on my lips. *Not bad.* I smiled at my reflection. I had on my vintage green turquoise earrings and a large matching pendant. A long light brown gypsy style skirt with small ruffles at the bottom and a white T-shirt and leather sandals completed the look I was going for. Casual, yet stylish, accessorized with lots of vintage turquoise jewelry is how I liked to describe my current dress code. After all, I needed a style of my own if I was dating.

I arrived at the coffee shop a little early. It was quiet inside with only two men at a table in the far corner. The delicious smell of coffee permeated the air. I had a book to read and grabbed my dark rimmed glasses out of my purse. Perfect look for a *coffee* date. I was pleased with myself that I had decided to come meet him.

The door flung open and a tall, thin well-dressed man rushed in. *That must be him* I thought. He was frantically looking around and I am not sure he even noticed me. I stood up to get his attention, smiled at him and started to say "Hi."

Before I could finish the greeting he looked at me and said, "I've left something in the car. I'll be right back." With that he dashed back out the coffee shop door.

I stood there for a moment and then sat back down at the table. *He is not coming back,* I thought. Then I started laughing. *How long should I wait to prove my point?*

A few minutes passed and I went up to the counter. "May I use your phone for a minute? I think my date just bolted on me." I had not yet purchased my trusty cell.

I called my best friend who I always keep posted on my whereabouts. She knew I was meeting someone and wanted the details as soon as I got home and could call. *Bet she's not expecting to hear from me so soon.*

"Well he ran in and ran out," I told her, giggling at the idiotic situation. "I don't think it was me, he never even looked at me." But there I was dressed quite cheeky and nowhere to go but home.

I made a quick run to the grocery store and then headed back to the house. It actually had felt good to get dressed up and drive out. I had no desire to really meet this man, but I did need an adventure to get me out of my empty house. So all in all, being the shortest date I've had so far, it was one of the best. The evening had all of the excitement leading up to the meeting and none of the stress of dealing with it. Maybe he was my kind of guy after all.

I never did find out what happened because he never called me back. But every so often I see him still on the dating site announcing *you will not meet another guy like me.*

And to that I say "Thank Heavens!"

Turning A Bad Date
Into A Dream Job

It was to be our second date, a first for me. No one rated number two for me and no one thought I passed muster for a second round either. Thursday night after dinner he suggested we see each other again on Saturday. I wasn't sure I liked him, but I liked the idea of Saturday.

"Saturday night is great," I grinned.

Finally, a Saturday night date. I have this old high school mentality about dating and Saturday night is the *only* night of the week that counts. I had arrived.

"Had lunch in mind," he corrected me. "And we can visit the botanical gardens, it's close by."

"Works for me," I answered him, grimacing at my error. "Where should we meet?"

Phooey, I grumbled to myself.

It was October and my luck on the dating services was not so hot. Sad news for a gal who once thought *she* was hot.

"Which sites have you tried?" a friend quizzed me.

"All of them I think. Was on several last month. Even peeked at the adult one. Too hot for me."

"What adult one? Aren't they all adults or did you plan on robbing the cradle again?" My girlfriend laughed at that one. A remark brought on by my telling her about the 30 year old high school coach who wrote me I was sexy. *Like an older sister*. He had some family issues somewhere I am sure.

"Adults. As in adults wanting to meet strangers for sex. Yucky. I went in and ran CC cleaner on my computer after that one. Made me feel like my computer could catch a virus from that site. For sure I would."

"So why keep trying. I don't get it." Why would she? She's got that cute husband at home.

"Yeah, the guys aren't so hot but it's fun to get out." I rolled my eyes thinking of all the frogs I've met. "Some real horn toads, or should I say *horny* toads?"

She laughs.

My karma really sucks at dating. I have more fun making jokes about the guys than I have meeting them. Maybe that is part of my problem. I think I want to date, but I really just want to fill some time.

I couldn't decide if I liked this latest match. He was in his early fifties, well dressed, sandy hair and dark glasses. He was about my height and had a nice build. His smile was a little crooked, but not as much as his nose was. The image in front of me was someone a mother might choose if she were picking a date for you.

We had our second date, lunch at a trendy Mexican restaurant. After a nice Margarita sitting on the porch enjoying the glorious fall weather we headed to the Atlanta Botanical Gardens.

"You know I haven't been here since the late '70s." It was hard to believe that much time had passed. "It was just a plot of dirt and a doublewide trailer then." I wasn't telling him anything he didn't know. He was a frequent visitor there.

How had I overlooked the gardens for all those years? I was just preoccupied with everything else in my life I guess. What I saw Saturday left me breathless. The changes were magnificent. It was a bit of heaven right in the heart of Atlanta. The gardens covered over

30 acres of land right next to Piedmont Park. A far cry from the dirt patch I had visited all those years ago. My heart relaxed and I smiled like an idiot. I felt at home in this beautiful sanctuary.

The day was perfect for October, cool and slightly overcast. Two exhibits were on display at the gardens that month. *Sculpture In Motion, Art Choreographed By Nature*, a display of metal sculptures that moved with the wind. It was stunning to see them mixed in with the beauty of the garden foliage. The breeze that day energized everything, especially me.

The other exhibit was *Scarecrows In The Garden*. The scarecrows were life-size Halloween characters created by individuals, designers and businesses. There were a hundred scarecrows placed throughout the garden, each with its own fantasy theme. My favorite, going back to my days with my realtor husband, was a huge display of grim reapers towering over a small plot of houses. Submitted by whom else? *Fannie Mae and Freddie Mac.* I made a note to check with the gardens to find out how to submit an application for a scarecrow. Maybe next year I could make one of my own.

I acted like a schoolgirl I know, but I was so excited I clasped my hands together, looked at my date and the words flew out of my mouth, "Oh promise me!"

"I don't make promises on second dates." His abrupt reply startled me.

I chose to ignore his remark. "I don't mean anything by that other than if we don't date, let's just be friends. I like to be friends with everyone."

"I'm sure you do," he was frowning as he spoke. "But I don't make promises I can't keep."

Shit, I thought. *What is it with this him?* I certainly hit a nerve with the word promise.

I never leave well enough alone. "Hey, I am not trying to be *When Harry Met Sally* and stay friends for years then fall in love, just friends now."

His reply was the final straw. "I am sure you are excited, so take this experience and make it into your own."

And that is the *second* thing I did. The first thing was to unload this guy as quickly as I could.

In the wee hours of the morning I went up to the Atlanta Botanical Gardens web site to volunteer my services. Their web page is magical. Flowers pop up as you scroll across the top, each opening with a list of information. I was looking for the word *volunteer* to appear when a bloom opened and beckoned me with the word *employment.* I followed my lead.

Part time sales associate. I smiled at that. Yes! Perfect for me with all my experience as an antique dealer. I immediately e-mailed my resume and included my photo.

Why the photo? Because I was worried being 60 and a widow sounded old. I still had not rid myself of the stigma of that word.

Within a week I was working at the gift shop. A bad date led me to a dream job. Another unexpected result from a dating service. The botanical gardens became my Prince Charming that day, not the date that had taken me there.

He couldn't make promises, but I could. I promised myself I would not give in to sorrow.

I kissed my computer and a feeling of well being came over me. Sometimes I feel I am being guided by a higher being and the dating services are my private chariot. I don't know where this ride is going, but I am moving along.

So Why Did You Leave Your Old Beau?

Did you know you can get a *wink* online? It doesn't compare to a *wink* across a crowded room or a *wink* from the cute bartender handing you a Margarita. But it does seem to be the current version of that old flirting technique.

All of the online dating services offer *winks*. On some, if you are a paying member you can e-mail a prospective date or you can send a little *wink*. That little *wink* puts the other person on notice they have been flirted with. Someone has found them interesting. Then they can *wink* back or send an e-mail to continue the process. They can just ignore it completely if they like, as I found out when I sent my own little *wink* to a hunk in North Carolina.

A few of the services let you look at members for free. You can't send a message if you don't join, but you can send a *wink*. Haven't figured out the reasoning behind that one. If you are not a paying member and you send a *wink* how will someone respond back? A total waste of time if you ask me. And personally, if someone is too cheap to join, I am worried about his free *wink*.

I find this very confusing. I am a cut to the chase kind of gal. If a male finds me alluring enough to send a *wink*, why can't he just write and say *hello*? Grow up out there guys. Where are the action men who take control? Taken, most likely by smart women.

I write this in my profile. *Do not send winks, I will not reply.* Yet *winks* as far away as California still come my way. I look for the day when someone will actually take the time to send a civilized message. I almost gave up hope of this and one afternoon there it is. A real message, not a *wink*.

Your personal e-mail is not given out, but the potential date writes to you through the dating service and they notify you *you've got mail*. The current dating service I am on has e-mailed me there is a message waiting when I log onto their site. Someone has written to me. *Thank heavens*, I think, *maybe this guy will be cool*.

I open his message. He has written, *So, why did you leave your old beau? I am sure he was a stand-up guy.*

Does this man not read? He got the part about no *winks*. But my profile clearly says *widow*. I don't look at his photo. I don't read his profile. I hit the reply button and send a message back.

Do you think I was too brunt? Too cruel? For I am sure this man will watch the next message he writes to someone.

Thanks for your note. I did not leave my old beau, he left me. He died.

Perhaps there are greetings worse than *winks* after all.

Those Questions I Dared To Ask, Condoms Anyone?

Condoms? What the hell do you do with condoms? Pretty sad to be 60 and have to ask that question. I remember jokes about filling them with water and bursting them like balloons as kids. I remember scenes in movies where teens went in to buy them at the drugstore and were embarrassed. I even remember in 1989 when my mother and I visited London a window decorator had used condoms as the theme for her Christmas display. (Now there was a reason for a jolly holly season.). But I don't remember ever using one, since I never did.

Shortly after my husband died an old male friend of 30 years met me for dinner. He is an attorney who works with nurses groups and gives lectures on women coming back into the dating field later in life. We had not seen each other in several years.

"You know, women your age coming out of long term relationships are the biggest risk for STDs," he said looking at me with concern. "All they remember was birth control and now there is so much out there most older women don't even think about."

I was eating pizza and almost choked on the bite I had just taken. Sexually Transmitted Diseases. How did I overlook that one? I swallowed the pepperoni and gave up trying to eat the rest.

"Maybe you'd like to come with me to one of my lectures? You can be my example." He actually smiled like this is a good idea. I looked at him like he had a third eye.

Well, I'd be mighty proud to be held up as an example for some things I thought, *but not this.*

"Think I'll pass on this one, kind sir." I gently kicked him under the table.

Condoms. This bleak aspect of dating made me ask the most outrageous questions of the men I went out with from the dating services. I wanted to know how men handled this issue. I would ask my questions and strangely enough I got answers. But there were no second dates.

"So," I asked one fellow on our first dinner date, "what do you do about condoms?"

His look told me he thought I was crazy but his smile said *OK, let's talk.* I got my answers and we got excellent service. It seems our waiter also wanted to hear what my date had to say.

"If I am in a committed relationship, I don't use a condom," he nodded at me as if to reaffirm his remark to himself.

That sounded fair, I thought. If only he had stopped there, but he continued.

"If I am seeing someone regularly but not exclusively, I don't use a condom with her, but I use one with any other girls I have sex with."

Oh my, who wouldn't want to be his special girl?

He seemed pleased with his answer and we finished our dinner. I made a note to mark him off my list as a future date.

"Need a refill on your coffee?" The waiter was back yet again, a silly grin on his face.

"Just the check, please," my date cut in, "and separate checks if you can."

As he said goodnight at my car he reached out to put his arms around me and steal a kiss. I jerked my head back.

"Shy." I was pleased my timing had cut him off. I didn't mind paying for my own dinner, but his answers to my questions killed my appetite for anything else.

"What about all that talk about condoms?" He seemed a bit confused.

"Oh, that?" I realized he probably thought I wanted to use condoms with him. *So not the point.*

"New to all this. Just curious." I gave him my sweetest smile. Yes, most likely I left him with the wrong impression with my questions, but inquiring minds have to know.

In the name of research I continued to ask that question and condoms became a part of my vocabulary but not a part of my life.

My next date was a 63-year-old widower who had been married for 34 years. We met for brunch at a New Orleans restaurant known for its French toast. It was twenty miles on the expressway from Decatur to the restaurant. I started to protest, but he assured me it was worth the drive. I assumed he was talking about the French toast. I did not need to haul my butt that distance for another strange man.

It was late November. A perfect Sunday morning with the sun so bright it hurt your eyes and the air so crisp you couldn't breath in enough of it. I was more excited about the drive than our meeting. The idea of a great brunch in a fancy restaurant on such a lovely day was all that I was interested in. I had my debit card tucked in my purse to pay for my brunch. Seems no male likes to pick up the tab while they are checking you out.

He was a nice looking man with grey hair, dressed in slacks and a blazer. He was very traditional looking in a suburban way. I wore jeans, ankle boots, a vintage leather jacket and lots of turquoise jewelry. My standard outfit it seemed for these casual dates.

"You have a bohemian look about you." He looked at me with curiosity.

We talked about dating since we had both lost our spouses that spring.

"I'd feel cheated if I fell in love right away," he told me while sipping on his mimosa. "I want to date a lot of women." I think he took it too seriously when a young girl who worked with him told him he was a good catch. He had visions of sex dancing in his brain.

"I want to learn about music," he continued. He thought music would help him open up, to feel things. His world had been an academic one as a research doctor. We talked about many things and after my second Bloody Mary I mentioned my condom worries to him.

Our brunch and conversation continued as I ate all of my French toast. It *was* worth the drive.

"So, if we date, what can you teach me?" he asked.

I got excited about that one. "I can teach you about music, art, antiques, flea markets, thrift stores and all the wonders of Atlanta's little neighborhoods." I felt quite pleased with myself. I had so much to offer.

"And what could you teach me?" I asked most sincerely.

His short reply, "How to use a condom."

My best friend brought a post card back from her recent trip to Thailand. She ate at a restaurant called *Cabbages and Condoms*. This restaurant is run by Thailand's Population and Community Development Association and promotes birth control. The postcard has an image of a heart made of multi colored condoms and reads, *No Glove, No Love*! I have it taped to the fridge as a reminder of all I have to look forward too.

The X-Rated Chapter

Ah yes, the world of instant messaging (IM). Who would believe that at age 60 I am on the computer at all hours of the night looking at the penis of a man I have never met? He is telling me his life story between sending me photos of his dick. The good part, he is 46 years old, a construction worker, very well built (at this point I should know) and a pleasure to look at. I am referring to his smiling face not his manly member.

"How do you know it was really his dick?" a girl friend of mine questioned me while having Margaritas with dinner.

My other friend joined in. "Maybe he was using someone else's photos."

I love to share my late night madness with the girls.

"It was his all right," I assured them.

"But how can you be so certain?"

"We met on a dating site and the photo of his face there was the same face as the one of him wearing jeans he sent me when we were IM." I thought that sounded pretty clear. *Or did it?*

"Well at least you know it was him with his clothes on." My one friend would not let it drop.

My first online dick shot. I can't believe my friends are drilling me on this. Trying to kill my magic moment.

"Did he talk dirty?" My married friend with her fantasy life.

"Stop it." My other friend has gently punched the married gal.

Then her attention is back to me. "Ok, so convince me it was his dick."

"That's simple." I felt smug answering them. "The bookcase in the background is the same in all his photos. From the dating site to his IM. Same lovely old blue bookcase. Great backdrop for a penis." An antique dealer does not miss details like that. *Who says I am not a romantic?*

"Did you send him any photos?" my friends grin at me.

"Hell, no." I shook my head. "Do you think I'm nuts? He knows what my face looks like from the dating site, that's all."

We were giggling like silly schoolgirls, perhaps one Margarita too many.

"How big was it?" My married friend is on a roll. "Did you wish you could see it in person?"

Hmmmm. There's a thought. Haven't seen a real one in awhile.

"You are crazy, but we love ya." I swear they said it in unison.

Yes, *crazy* just about sums it up. All this talk about instant messaging and I wanted to be a part of it, or at least find out what all the commotion was about. I downloaded a popular instant messaging service at the suggestion of a 35 year old friend of mine from work.

"You'll love it," he told me. "Your friends can tell if you are online and you can hook up with each other."

Instant messaging, for those like me who didn't know, is chatting in real time on the Internet as you type messages back and forth. You don't send e-mails and have to wait for a reply. You just type your message and the other person gets it and writes right back. Most of the time there is a flickering note at the bottom of your monitor that tells you a reply is being written. You can send photos and if you have a web-cam you can send instant videos. I couldn't wait to try it!

The construction worker and I had been sending e-mails through the dating service for over a week. He lived somewhere up North, so our chances of meeting were slim. His stories entertained me and he answered all my prodding questions. Such as, "If some of your friends are transsexuals, are you straight or bi?" Well, he brought up the subject. He also told me he was dating an old married girlfriend who didn't like sex with her husband as much as she did with him. Hey, true or false, at 1AM it was interesting.

Finally he wrote, can you *IM?*

Why yes I can, I excitedly e-mailed back. We hooked up and started chatting away, typing funny things to each other and flirting outrageously. It was so much easier being able to write back and forth, rather than wait for all the e-mails to arrive.

Want to see some photos? He wrote me.

Sure, my immediate reply. I'd like to see more of his face. See if he really is that handsome. How naïve was that?

The first photo was of him standing in the room dressed in jeans. Pretty darn cute. A second photo came in of his smiling face and bare chest. A nice chest with the slightest bit of dark curly hair.

Oh my, I thought.

When did you take that photo? I wrote back.

Just now, getting ready for bed, his quick response. The next photo he sent was of his mid section and he had started to unzip his jeans.

Better stop, I may faint, I quickly wrote him. *Sleep tight, we'll catch up later.*

You are so cute. I believe he is referring to my remark and not how great I look. Either works for me. At sixty I like being called cute by anyone.

His final message to me that night, *talk soon.*

I leaned back in my chair staring at the monitor. *Now that was something,* I smiled. Then hastily shut down the computer for the night.

Several nights later while checking out an auction site on the computer his message popped up. *Hi cutie.*

Oh good, he's back, I thought. I was in a flirting mood. It had been a long day and I was feeling lonely. This would be fun. Tonight I was ready for him.

Hi Cutie, yourself, what's up? I typed back quickly. *Maybe his dick.* I toyed with that idea.

We actually chatted for some time. He talked about going to an art gallery opening and a play over the previous weekend. I talked about watching movies on TV and grooming the dogs. I was at my boredom limit when he wrote me that night.

Want some more photos? He typed. *Got the camera here.*

I knew what was coming and thought *why the hell not?*

Sure, send 'em on. I hit reply.

Four photos came in, one after another, starting with another body shot of him fully dressed. The other three photos were of his dick taken at various angles. It wasn't until the third horizontal shot that I realized it really was a penis. The camera angle is everything in a photo.

Like it? I'm getting hot sending these to you.

You are hot, I flirt back.

I am smiling to myself. He thinks he is turning me on and I *know* he is getting turned on. His photos tell me so. Me? I am just plain curious. Who does this sort of thing? And how crazy am I to be enjoying it? I am even critiquing his writing like an old school mistress pleased his grammar is better than mine. I seem more excited about that painted bookcase than his nude penis. *Is that a good thing or a bad thing?* I take a sip of sherry and raise my glass in the air. "A toast to technology." I am talking to my walls.

He is slow with the camera. I wonder if he is also sending photos to someone else. Maybe his penis is making the rounds. But I don't ask that question. Waiting for him to take the photos has given me time to walk the dogs and get my bottle of sherry from the pantry. I am keeping an eye on my monitor as I go about my business. Hate to miss anything tonight.

I smile and take another sip of sherry and type a message to him.

Oh yes, send another photo. I coax him on. *Can you move the camera a little to the right? And hold it steady. Last one was blurry.*

I know I will be deleting the instant messaging program tomorrow, but for tonight I want to play.

It is harmless. Safe sex at its best. And I have saved one of his penis photos on my computer's hard drive. It will truly be the erection that lasts for more than four hours.

You Can Get A Man With A Gun

Oh my, maybe I am showing my age. Using lyrics from the musical *Annie Get Your Gun* to tell you about a man I met. And I don't even like musicals. But I sure like Annie Oakley. The cowgirl I want to be.

I believe Annie Oakley laments, "Oh you can't get a man with a gun." Well I did, kinda, and with a load of shot packed in the rear of my van to boot.

I liked him the minute his photo popped up as a match. His looks melted me. He was 58, about 6 feet tall, sandy hair and a short beard. The type of man that is handsome but with an earthy rugged look. His eyes crinkled as he smiled and I knew we had to meet.

His voice was deep with a hearty chuckle when we talked on the phone the next day. "Joined this some months back while I was looking for my office," he told me. "Just started a new business and my free time is pretty much gone now."

In addition to the work schedule from hell he lived miles away in a small town outside the Atlanta beltway. So logistically he was going to be hard to catch up with and he had no time to come my way. My mind was searching for something to make this click and then he gave me my opening.

"I shoot skeet," he told me. "Reload my own shells and teach kids gun safety."

"You shoot skeet?" I was getting excited. "So did my Dad. I have all his old reloading equipment and my late husband's guns." I failed to mention I know nothing of guns.

"Guns," he replied in surprise. "Nothing in your profile shows you like guns."

Full of surprises, that's me.

Then the invite I wanted. "You should come down here and let me take you to dinner and show you the old Olympic shooting range."

After my husband died I found we had a small arsenal in the house. I had no idea how to get rid of it and I didn't want to advertise it for sale. That would be an announcement to the world of mad men I was living alone. How crazy would that make me? Crazier than I appear to be now, that's a certainty.

"Would you like me to bring you my Dad's skeet stuff?" I asked him. "I need to get this out of the house and maybe you can use it for the kids." I actually like for family things to go on to a new life helping someone else rather than to sell them.

I heard the excitement in his voice. "Hell yes, bring it down!"

The sun was shining brightly as I loaded my van. I worked up a bit of a sweat. I hauled an old reloader, bullets, empty shells, bags of shot and a box or two of ancient gunpowder out of the basement. I kept the guns. I tossed an old quilt over everything and headed out. I felt like Annie Oakley with a van full of ammo going to meet her man.

As I got on the interstate I thought, *please don't let me get stopped for speeding.* I took a quick look at the back of the van and thought *shit, if I'm stopped I'll go straight to jail.* I grabbed my cell and gave him a quick call. "On my way, if I am not there in an hour, check the 6 o'clock news!" Then I relaxed, turned on the radio and hit it.

I think I decided to have sex with him on the drive to see him. I know sex was on my mind after hearing his voice. Or maybe it was that twinkle in his eye when he said hello and gently touched my arm that made me think of sex. But when he laughed that deep throaty laugh of his as he unloaded my van and saw what I had hauled down the expressway I knew I wanted him.

I arrived earlier than he expected because I didn't want to get caught in rush hour traffic. He was still working. He offered me a glass of wine, squeezed my hand and pointed to the stairs. "Go up and make yourself comfortable and I'll see you soon." He lived above his office.

A huge bed greeted me as I entered the room. The TV was on so I kicked off my shoes, got up on the bed and positioned myself to look mysteriously sexy for his arrival. I was so comfortable on his bed that I fell asleep waiting for him. His pillows had the smell I no longer had on my pillows at home. I don't know if it is sweat or just hair oil, but there was that ever so faint odor I remembered from the days I had my husband in bed with me. I hugged the pillow and felt the warm breeze filter through the windows and felt at home in a stranger's house.

He gently woke me and smiled down at me. "Let's get some pizza," he said as he reached to caress my head. I reached out for him, hungry for something and it was not pizza. We fell into lovemaking as naturally as two people who knew each other well.

The evening was perfect, as though written in a romance novel. He was as sexy as I thought he would be and his lovemaking was exactly what I needed. Afterwards we did go for that pizza and he held my hand as we walked down the street like old sweethearts. The railroad track ran across one side of town as it does in many small southern towns. The stars were bright in the sky and he said hello to all the people we passed on the way to dinner. A small town with all the quaintness and charm you would expect.

After dinner he put his arms around me. "Stay the night," he whispered in my ear.

"Can't." I shook my head. "Have to get back to the dogs."

The truth was I wanted to have sex with him, but I was not ready to wake up in a new man's bed. Somehow sex did not seem as intimate as spending the night and I was not ready for that familiarity.

I still have my husband's two guns and wonder if I will finally learn how to shoot them. I have this vision, it is chilly afternoon and I am wearing jeans, a vintage leather jacket, cowboy boots and my turquoise jewelry. My concealed weapons permit is tucked in my tooled leather Mexican handbag. I drive to a shooting range in my 79 Stingray and walk in to find a handsome cowboy who will teach me how to finally load my guns. Guns and guys, what is it with them. But then, I like guys with guns, what is it with me?

The Widow Rule

Just the other day I was having a glass of wine with a pudgy young man. You got it, another online match. I thought to myself looking at him, his mouth moving endlessly telling me something I was not paying attention too, *how did I wind up dating again after all these years?* This is a question I always seem to ask myself every time I have a bad date.

The answer is always the same. *Oh yes, I remember, my husband died.* How inconsiderate was that? Of all the things he did over the years we were together this was definitely the most thoughtless. Not like forgetting a birthday or anniversary. He left me right as I was passing over into the next decade. Sixty.

Age is just a state of mind self help books tell you. Well my mind is freaking out. Hell of a time to start all over again. I felt young, looked young, but for some reason everyone wanted to e-mail jokes to me about old age. I hate that.

A man my age said over our first and only coffee date, "Women your age are trying to grab anyone to marry for that final stretch."

Women my age. Right there I should have left. But I hung around for the biscotti.

I have discovered that men my age don't really like me. I am too blunt and not easily impressed. Besides, most of them are looking for younger gals. I find that amusing since they can't keep up with me, but think they can with someone younger. I dance circles around most of the men I meet.

My needs are simple. "Can you stay up past midnight?" I ask.

Haven't gotten a yes to that yet over coffee. Frankly I find men age appropriate for me too old for me. So the new phrase for older women with younger men is *cougar*. Perhaps that could be me I decided. The company of a younger man might be the tonic I need.

Tonight was my first younger male date. Age 49. I had high expectations but they deflated quickly. We met for dinner at a lovely pub close to my house and a good stiff drink was the only exciting thing in front of me. Watching paint dry had more appeal than the young man at my table. I take a slug of my Margarita and bring my attention back to him. He is waving his hand and making some remark so perhaps I should listen. I lean closer to him and twirl a strand of my hair and smile sweetly at him. You know that smile that says you are fascinating, especially after a nice strong drink. He was saying something about he viewed life as a glass half empty, rather than half full. See what I mean about dull?

However, what he said next peaked my interest.

"A friend of mine is getting married and his children are not talking to him anymore." Okay, a bit of gossip even if I didn't know the parties involved. "Yeah, his wife died less than a year ago. He started dating and now is getting married."

Well good for him, I think. *Life is for the living* is what everyone has told me. Boy am I a little sick of hearing that one.

"So what is the problem?" I have to know and this is the only thing interesting he has to offer on our date.

"It's the rule. He broke it." My young companion went on to explain it is a known fact that you are not to date for one year and one day after your spouse dies. It is a time of showing respect. Anything short of that is not proper. His friend didn't wait and now his children despise him for cheating on his dead wife.

"Is that so?" I am slightly horrified at the thought that there is some unknown time frame on these things floating in the universe that I am unaware of.

"I've never heard of that rule. They say it might take a year to start to pull together, a time for all the seasons to pass." I looked him straight in the eyes, challenging his remark.

"Oh, yes," he continues smug with authority. "An old Southern rule, my grandparents told me. One year and a day."

I look carefully at this unpleasant young man. My dating profile says *widow*, perhaps he missed that bit of information. In the short time since my husband died I have not only dated, but have had sex. I have most certainly broken the sacred rule.

I talk about dating all the time with friends and co-workers. Now I am worried maybe they know about this rule and are judging me. "Look at her, husband dead not a year and she is dating and sleeping around." I can almost hear them talking behind my back. "Must not have been a happy marriage." The very thought makes me sick.

I look around quickly and see our waiter. My hand shoots up flagging him to our table. "Check please," I say, surprising my companion. "Have to feed the dogs," I smile at him with all the charm I can muster. "Please let me get home," I pray to the god of bad dates.

This horrid young man, who is so sure he is right on the rules that govern spouses who have lost spouses, has now got me questioning myself. Bad enough I am depressed over my husband's death, now I can be paranoid too. But his statement does have me wondering, am I an *unfaithful widow*?

Counting Xanax
Instead Of Sheep

No Dog Biscuits and no Xanax. Talk about a shit night. Not a moment's peace. I couldn't sleep and the dogs were anxiously looking for their usual bedtime treats.

"Babies, it was raining so hard." I try to console my dogs. They are not to be convinced. "Hell, you won't even go outside to pee in the rain." I am glaring back at Foxy and then to Jake who is laying on his mat looking at me intently. "Why should I want to stop at the store in this downpour?"

That made perfect sense to me. But the dogs appeared disgruntled without their evening treats. Foxy turned to walk into the sunroom and I think she mooned me raising her tail high as she trotted out. Talk about attitude. Jake was a prisoner in the dining room, unable to get off his mat but continued to look hopeful. "Sorry, sweetie." I felt badly for Jake. But nothing was sending me into that rain again.

"Damn." I looked down at my soaked skirt. There was a sudden cloudburst as I left the gardens a little earlier. My umbrella was up, but the wind and rain came at me in horizontal torrents soaking everything but my head. Clear through to my panties. The reason I didn't stop before coming home was that my skirt was clinging to me showing every curve of my behind. Not the most becoming look for me.

I stripped down quickly and hung my skirt to dry over the tub. Then I slipped into dry undies and my long man's T-shirt that says *Road Kill*. Exactly how I am feeling tonight. It is one of my husband's old shirts. Sometimes it feels good to wear something of his at night. I don't wear nightgowns anymore, but usually sleep in a long shirt of some sort. It is one of my widow changes. I can slide my jeans on quickly if I have to run a dog out.

Sipping a small glass of sherry, I'm watching some sappy romantic movie on TV where two people meet on a dating service and fall madly in love. "Right." I snorted so hard sherry flew up my nose.

"Tell it like it is," I shout at the TV. "Losers, all losers."

Hmmm, maybe I've had a little too much sherry. But what the hell. If you can't poke fun at stupid movies, what is the sense of watching them? I'd give anything for one of my favorite movies tonight. Snuggle under my quilt, drink a little, and sigh at what Hollywood is telling me romance can be like. *But, no, I've just got dribble to watch.*

The dogs have settled down. Sleeping peacefully. I am pleased with myself that I did not give in to their pitiful looks and run back out for biscuits. "No problemie." I am delirious with happiness or maybe sherry.

Time to call it a night, I decide. It's still early for me, but the day has exhausted me. Most nights I take a half of Xanax to help me sleep. Otherwise no matter how tired I am, thoughts stray to my husband and I stay up all night. Anxiety attacks that take me from feeling relaxed to watching the clock hands move slowly hour to hour.

I brush my teeth, gargling a little, as I get ready for the final rinse. I've filled my frog mug with water so I can have some left for my pill. I reach for my Xanax container and as I lift it there is no sound. No rattling of pills. *Oh shit.* That was the other thing I was to do after work, get dog biscuits and my prescription refill. Now it is too late to dress and head back out. I drag to bed wondering how long this evening will be.

The dogs are sleeping soundly. Their moment of stress over no bones has passed. Mine is just beginning. No pills, no sleep. *Shit, shit, shit.*

I flop into bed and pull the covers up before reaching to the bedside table for the lamp. Foxy who sleeps by my bed has raised her head. *Has she heard me? Do I detect a slight smile on her face as she hears me wailing over my Xanax?* She gets up off her mat and twirls around making herself comfortable in another spot. I hear a little sigh as she plops back down. Is she showing me how easily she can sleep? Repayment for not having her evening biscuits. God how rude is that?

I click off the light and rest my head on the soft pillow. Then I wait. Wait for sleep. Sleep that doesn't come. I glance across the room and stare at the clock. In my head all I can hear is *tick,tock, tick,tock.* And with every moment that passes I am counting Xanax pills instead of sheep.

Dating Blues Poem

Mirror, Mirror, On The Wall
Who Do I See, If Anyone At All?
Thought I was once so cute and perky,
But all my dates are making me feel jerky.

My husband was such a handsome man
Now meeting creeps as fast as I can.
Not smart, not cute, not pleasing, nor witty
So many dull men, it is such a pity.

Bald ones, old ones, young ones too
Only thing on their minds, they want to screw.
Doesn't any one remember it's nice to be friends?
But on that word a date usually ends.

Is it too much to ask for someone who's nice?
Then maybe add to it a spoonful of spice.
But they all try to kiss and make a big pass,
Oh my, some even try to grab boobs and your ass.

Not worthy of kisses, most are horn toads,
And I'm finding at any age, they are all old.
Whether 40 or 60 they all act the same,
Tired, worn out, please hand them a cane.

No man, however great he tells me he is,
Can't beat my energy, his is a fizz.
Can't stay up late to try and have fun,
The clock ticks 9, it's bedtime, gotta run.

Unless it's my bed he is heading for,
But early to bed to me such a bore,
I like to play the same as most men,
But only late, and if I say when.

I am sixty, and run like a fawn.
Up all hours til the break of dawn.
My day is as full as the hours at night,
And gee, no sleep, and I am still bright.

So mirror, please tell me is there's any hope
That maybe I'll meet someone that's not a dope?
Spoiled by the man who I finally married,
And maybe a torch for him I still carry.

Is it me? Is it them? I often question.
For with dating, I have no sense of direction.
The judgment I face by those lesser men,
Deciding if I am good enough for them.

They miss the point, they think they are cool.
To me, each one is his own little fool.
One day as in every fairy tale, I am told
You may be rescued by a prince who is bold.

My prince will know I don't need to be saved,
For life has taught me how to be brave.
Two princes in a lifetime, two men who I love
Will be a blessing I'll get from the man up above.

In the meantime I have a life of my own
Music to make, my own little song.
Dancing to the rhythm of life
Remembering once I was a great wife.

Super Widow

It all boils down to this. I am tired. Beat up tired, emotionally tired, drained. My fizz has gone flat. Too exhausted to even think about sex. *OMG, now I know I am tired.*

This is not necessarily a bad thing. It proves that I am alive. My heart is still beating and I am moving, sometimes backwards and sometimes forwards. As long as I am not stationary, glued in place by fear, I can handle tired. But my energy level at keeping myself busy has depleted me.

Running like a mad woman to be the *I can do it all female.* To be the widow who has made a life for herself.

Super Widow. I think I'll get a T-shirt made.

Life has always been this hectic for me; don't let my whining fool you. I just didn't have so much social activity squeezed into the picture. I'd run myself ragged during the day and come home to relax with my husband at night.

I didn't have to wonder if there was a man to have sex with that I'd still like to see in the morning. Dating. The hardest work I've done and it pays less than minimum wage.

"So why keep dating?" This is my friend's response to my latest grumblings. We are out eating our favorite nachos.

Before I can answer she answers for me. "You have to keep dating or who will keep me laughing with their horror stories?"

"Glad to be so entertaining." I am smiling at her.

But there is that dating question again. *Why still do it?* I always talk about my dates. Most days it makes me laugh. Some days it is not so funny. Today my brain is screaming, *stop asking me why.* I wonder if I said this or just thought it. *Shit.* Don't want to be rude. I'm just tired. I look at my friend and she hasn't heard anything. I'm safe.

How do you explain that it's really not about the men for me but my mission to keep moving forward. Maybe I'll meet someone, maybe I won't. That it's about the date itself. My fear that if I stop thinking about it the game will be over. I will become too comfortable where I am. I need to stay in practice.

I am a people watcher. Everyone fascinates me. I like to hear their stories. Men and women.

Dating, such a rude awakening. What a shock to discover the guy across the table from me is checking his watch to move on while I am trying to see if he has something special to add to our conversation.

I've finally admitted to myself I don't have to like everyone and they don't have to like me. It's cool. It's liberating. Sometimes it's a blessing. I am referring to men here. The women I meet are hip, smart and talented. It is such a shame none of us are gay. Life would be easier now.

The men? You tell me.

"You are not nearly as much fun as I'd hoped." I was told by my dinner date who was taking medication for severe depression.

"I'm very private and you have violated my trust issues." A farewell e-mail from a man I had never met in person, but told me all about his family. I asked a question he didn't like and I was deleted.

"I just don't feel the chemistry," a final call from a man in his late sixties you couldn't pay me to have sex with, dismissing me for not appealing to him.

A hot young guy who shared a few Margaritas with me at happy hour then dropped me off at home, his parting words as he drove off, "If you decide to sell the Corvette, call me."

The man who called himself a gentleman in his profile and stated he was separated from his wife. I returned his call and he hung up the phone saying, "Don't call unless I say you can." When we talked again he said his wife had been there.

"Oh was she picking up some of her things?" I was curious on that one.

"No, she lives here," his answer.

"Well how are you separated?" Now I really want to know.

"We sleep in separate bedrooms. Haven't had sex in three years."

"Does she know you're separated?"

"We don't talk about it."

She was out of town visiting the grand kids and he wanted to have some fun. I really didn't like him. He made my *you make my skin crawl* list.

Then there was the cowboy, complete with duster and boots who had horses on a farm south of Atlanta. We were to meet at the Scott Antique show on the same side of town where he lived. I got a call from him just as I was heading out. "Did you know the price of gas is up a dollar a gallon, I can't afford to meet you." His final remark during that conversation, "I am really looking for a woman to help work the ranch." *Yippee-ki-yay!*

Perhaps my favorite was the tango dancer. I took my best friend to the restaurant he held dancing classes at once a month. We had dinner then went to check on the dancing. He was in his mid sixties, black hair that had a curl at the top, a stomach hanging over his belt, and was my height. Dancing was his passion. He grabbed me for a twirl on the dance floor and I had two left feet. I found the tango an uncomfortable dance. You lean on your partner and move your legs backwards. My chest was on his gut and I was getting leg cramps. I sat the next few dances out while he danced with my friend and some other females. When he asked me to try again, I had to say "No thanks." The next day I got an e-mail from him. *While it was nice to meet you, we are not a match. You do not take the Tango seriously.*

I must not leave out the older gentleman who was the reason I decided to exit the dating services for a while. I grabbed my morning cup of coffee, sat down at the computer and brought in my e-mails. I was greeted with a photo of a 72 year old man, dressed in shorts, strutting his naked chest. The message from the dating service cheerfully telling me he wanted to meet me. *Oh so not what I want to wake up to in the morning!* Delete!

Dating, so humorous and so exhausting. I think I will sleep for a week and then start all over again. After all, my married girl friends count on my stories to entertain them, to remind them of the wonderful single life they are missing.

We all need super heroes in our lives, not just in the movies. Someone to rescue us, someone who is extraordinary and can make things better, someone to save us in the face of life's dangers and pitfalls, someone who is daring and full of adventure. Most super heroes on the big screen are men ready to rescue the damsel in distress. But this is real life and it calls for a plan of action to be ready to greet each day. No one to rescue me. I will be my own super hero, Super Widow.

Winter

*You're just jealous because
the voices only talk to me.*

Hello, Anyone There?

Some folks have asked me, "Have you gotten a sign from your husband yet?" That question makes me very nervous. You'd be surprised how many times it comes up. That question is usually followed with, "They come to you in dreams, you know." Others have said to me, "Sometimes it's through electrical things that they try to get your attention."

A widower I met said his wife contacted him right after her death. He was watching TV and a light flickered in the bathroom. He went to check on it and could smell her perfume heavy in the air. He was convinced she was saying goodbye on her way to a better place.

Maybe I am not looking hard enough I decide. I need to open up and see if my husband is trying to make contact with me. I have been watching and waiting. Small irregularities in the house now make me wonder *is he here?*

The first few months after my husband died the computer started shutting itself off some nights while I slept. My husband always turned the computer off before heading to bed. I on the other hand leave it on all the time. I'd wake in the morning and see the dark black monitor and think, *is that you, honey?*

Two questions crossed my mind. *Is he trying to contact me?* Or, *is he pissed I am leaving his computer on?* He was very protective of his computer. It was his favorite toy. Now it is my favorite toy and I am doing all the things he said not to do with it.

Every morning for the next month I would slowly come down the long hallway from the bedroom to the office, anxious to see if the computer had turned off. Many mornings it had. I'd sit at the computer, coffee in my hand and wonder, *is that my sign?* Then I'd shake my head reminding myself how silly that was and would go about my business. But it stayed on my mind.

One day I finally asked my best friend for her opinion. "Do you think he is turning off the computer at night?"

This is why I love my best friend, she grounds me in reality.

"What are you nuts?" She looked at me in disbelief. "Something is probably wrong with your computer."

She reached in her purse and pulled out a card. "Call Rick, Bee Tree Tech, my computer guy."

So now her computer guy is my computer guy.

"You know, the computer shuts itself off a lot at night and I need someone to take a look at it." I called him, giving him my widow saga. "My husband's old computer. He maintained it. I am a dolt with what to do."

He is the best. Came over that day to check it out. I couldn't resist the temptation to share my theory.

"Some of my friends tell me it could be a sign from my husband. He's shutting it down at night."

Now computer guy is very aware of my level of competence with a computer and perhaps my mental state.

After working on it for a short while he found the problem. "Fans gone bad, your computer is overheating and turning itself off."

Oh my, is that all? I thought. Instead of being joyful the problem was small, I was sad it wasn't contact from the other side.

He replaced the fan and reset the alarm on the computer to let me know if it overheats. "It should be fine now."

I wrote him a check. Tucked his card away safely for the future. But I have to admit I haven't had any more *signs* from my husband on the computer since.

I use the food timer for my morning alarm. It is so much easier than the actual alarm clock across the room. When it rings I know I am done and take myself out of bed. It has a softer sound than the alarm and Foxy appreciates that. She sleeps in the bedroom and hates to be disturbed.

I started noticing the timer was on a countdown at night when I went to bed. I knew I had turned it off in the morning. *Was this a sign?* I wondered. *Or am I just an idiot that can't work a food timer?* I am still thinking on that one. If I could only find the instructions for the timer I might get my answer.

Sometimes my dogs bark in my direction as though taken un-awares. I figured it was the darkness in the room, the shadows play-ing tricks when I walked in before I turned on the lights. Now I wonder if the dogs are seeing something I am not. It is a comforting thought that my husband may be appearing around me in a form only the dogs can see. I always say, "Hi, honey." Then I take a quick look behind me. Nothing. My attention turns to the dogs. "*Whaaat?*" But they are just wagging their tails hoping for bones.

My husband and I used to watch movies together at night. His favorites were fast paced action thrillers or science fiction. He did not like chick flicks and the only way he would watch a movie with a baby was if it turned out to be an alien child projecting from a stom-ach. On the rare occasion I would sneak in a romantic girly movie. One night we watched "Ghost", that movie with Patrick Swayze and Demi Moore, where he is protecting her from the other side. My husband actually liked that movie, but to my surprise it upset me.

Truth is, I can't handle the thought of two people in love sepa-rated by death and the one on the other side is still watching, want-ing to communicate. My husband knew that. So maybe that is why there aren't any signs.

My husband's cousin in California was a bit of a psychic and had many friends that were professionals in that field. Intuitive counselors. I met one of her friends at the Atlanta airport during her layover on the way to Costa Rica. She was delightful in person but her conversation unnerved me. We talked about my husband. She saw him confused and told me I needed to talk to him, to reassure him, to help him find his way. "Light a candle," she told me as she gently touched my arm.

She was trying to be helpful, but I got home that night and was upset. I didn't know what to believe. I do know how peaceful my husband looked the night he died and in my mind he was at rest.

But I thought if I needed to do something I would. So I lit a candle and started talking to my husband. Tears that I had pushed aside began to surface. I was so nervous I started to giggle. Then I began laughing. This is how I handle being uneasy. I finally decided if my husband was confused, it was because he was looking at the house wondering where the hell his things went.

"You know, honey, remember all those years ago I told you if you left me I'd fill the house with my things?" Then I blew out the candle. "Well, this is your fault."

I am open to most anything and still look for signs. I still talk to my husband and most mornings have me greeting him with a *hello* as I greet the dogs. And every time I put another nail in the wall I whisper, "Sorry, hon, but I really love this painting." I like to give him a hard time like I always did. Keeps things on an even keel.

Question For God

Dear God,

Did I die? Did I miss it? The psychic told me my husband was dead for two days before he knew he had died. I laughed that off. But maybe it is true. Geez. Is that it? I just haven't realized it yet?

That would explain everything. I've been home all day and the phone has not rung once. No e-mails. No human contact. Yes, the dogs see me, but don't dogs see ghosts anyway? They are sensitive and hear and see things we don't.

I wonder how I died? Must have been quick. Yesterday I was out with friends for dinner. Oh my, food poisoning? That would explain it. Friends saw me last night. No one knows I'm gone yet. But the food I ate killed me. I never knew Nachos could be deadly.

I've been asleep most of the afternoon. Needed a nap. On my husband's old couch, the death bed so to speak. I had a wonderful dream that my husband was by my side. He was smiling at me. He actually said these words. "House looks nice, honey." That snapped me awake. Still foggy, I look around. Am I in heaven? My husband likes the house. I must be in heaven. At least I didn't go to hell.

But it is so strange, God. Everything is the same around me. No clouds, no spirits. Just me and the dogs. And I am drinking a diet soda. But why, why hasn't anyone called? Not even a wrong number. No spam in my e-mails. I hit the send and receive key and nothing comes in. Wow, that Internet does know it all. How did the spammers know I was dead before anyone else?

I must be in limbo it is too quiet. I know I am dead. Is that right, God? And just where are those pearly gates?

Is that the phone ringing? I run and grab it.

Cautiously I say "Hello."

I wait, afraid of who is on the other end. I am sure I am dead. God, it better not be the devil asking where I am.

"Well you're home," my best friend on the other end. "Thought you were working today or I'd have called earlier."

"Yeah, just took a nap, had an odd dream, but now I'm hungry. Wanna go for dinner?"

That's it! How silly of me. I took the day off from work and told no one. No one expected me to be home. *Note to myself,* and help me to remember it, God. I actually write this down on a post it. *Don't panic so quickly when no one calls.*

I am still alive! Thank you God. Forgive me for questioning you on that. I should have known you would not have invited me into heaven, only to ignore me like those bad dates I've had. You would have greeted me in person, a true gentleman.

With my sincere apology,

Thankful I am still among the living,
The Widow Barbara

Those Girlfriends Of Mine

"*Do you* want to see someone, a counselor, a therapist? Someone to talk with about all this?" the nurse asked me. "It's that time of year when even normal people get depressed."

I called my doctor's office that morning worried about my blood pressure. I felt my throat and swore it was pulsating rapidly under my fingers. I definitely was anxious, she was right about that one. My first holiday alone quickly approaching.

"Even normal people…" I couldn't let that one slip by. "I'm normal, aren't I?"

We both laughed on that one. I didn't get an answer.

The nurse is a friend of mine. Actually I feel that way about both nurses in my doctor's office. They take the time to talk to me when I call. I'd like to think it was special treatment for me, but they just may be that special to everyone. He has a small office right down the street from my house so it is easy for me to pop in with every little symptom that crosses my mind.

"I'll be fine. Just got worried for a sec." I give her a small hug. "Bet you didn't realize that when I became a widow I also became a hypochondriac."

I laugh about that one but it is somewhat pitifully true. I never worried about my health when my husband was alive, but suddenly I feel the need to check on everything. Who would take care of the dogs if I got sick?

"So how is the antique business?" my friendly nurse asked. See what I mean? I left the doctor's office feeling great. Nothing was wrong with me that a little human contact couldn't cure.

Girlfriends, women friends, gal pals, Mother and sister, I have the best. They are the reason I don't need a therapist. Why pay money for a shrink when you have that kind of support system?

As with every ad on TV about a prescription drugs and their disclaimers on potential side effects that make you wonder why to take the drug at all, I must include my own disclaimer here. Serious depression does need help and shouldn't be ignored. I was dog down depressed over the loss of my husband and found that friends were my answer. I'd rather chat from my own couch on my cell or meet for drinks. That was the cure for what ailed me, loneliness.

My best friend is an old friend. I like to remind her she is six years older than me. We've been growing older together for as long as I knew my husband. She hasn't aged in looks in all those years. However, her age is something I play with.

"That guy that e-mailed me for a date is 66 years old. He's just too darn old for me."

"Shit, I'm 66," she replies, a little challenge in her voice.

"Well I wouldn't want to date you either."

Busted!

I don't call it dating, but we eat out a lot. I call her way too many times a day and she was my lifeline to sanity when my husband died. She is a chef, a world traveler, a photographer and has a studio where she makes incredible glass beads. Quite different from me, the pizza delivery gal, the one who rarely drives outside the Atlanta beltway known as 285. I am making my own jewelry, but nothing like hers. Vintage pieces recycled with bugs, toads and puppy dog tails. But she inspired me to try.

Another old friend, that word *old*, not meant in age but in time together, is an antique dealer. I started out as her customer drooling over all the beautiful things she sold. We decided to set up together at the Lakewood Antique Show and our friendship took off. We still meet weekly for lunch at our favorite Mexican restaurant in Lilburn, Georgia close by Antiques In Old Town, where she is a dealer. Put that shop on your GPS ladies.

She is three months older than me to the day. Her birthday is May 21st and mine is August 21st. She turned sixty first. *How pleased that made me.*

We tried to outdo each other about our upcoming birthdays last spring.

"God, I'm old," she lamented over tacos and iced tea. "Going to be sixty next month."

"Don't bitch to me," I stuffed my face with chips and salsa. "I'll be sixty and a widow. So I win this pity party."

"Besides," I continued, "I remember that boy toy cashier at the grocery store, when you asked for your senior discount he said no way, not with that Madonna thing you've got going with your hair."

She does have hair like Madonna.

"Okay, you win, now pass the damn chips."

Guess what, she'll be sixty-one before me too. Can't wait.

The antique world filled my life with wonderful women for years. Women of all ages. I say women because I have found that some females do not like to be called girls.

"I can't believe you said that word." One woman startled me as I was talking to a group at a local pub, her wine glass stopped mid air.

Shit, I thought. *Did I just say the F word?*

"Girl," she jumped back in my face. "You said girl. We've come too far to be called girls. What's wrong with being an adult? Being a woman?"

"Well, my friends are fun loving, smart, and savvy. Sure, they're women, but girls at heart." I couldn't believe I was having this conversation. "You can call me what you want, but please don't call me ma'am." I felt quite sassy with my reply. But God, how I hate being called ma'am. Now that makes me feel old.

She mellowed a little on that one. Maybe she will become a girlfriend down the road. We run in the same book club circles.

Two more girlfriends had me smuggling small bottles of wine into the movie theater the night *Sex In The City* had its premier.

The phone rang three different times. I was napping. I finally picked it up on the fourth call.

"Barbara, get up now. *Sex In The City*, remember? Picking you up in twenty minutes."

I splashed water on my face, a bit of powder and my lipstick and a fluff of my flat hair and I looked human again. Ready on time for the movie.

"Grab a bottle," my friend was handing me a small cooler as she backed out of my drive.

"Wine?"

"Hell yes, honey. We can buy popcorn at the theater."

I grabbed a small chardonnay. Felt quite naughty drinking later in the theater.

The three of us have known each other in the antique world for years but only since my husband's death have we gotten social. What a rescue team they are.

The one gal is dark haired, beautiful and married since her early days in school. "Tell me about the dates," she pushes at me. "What about sex? I want to hear all about it."

She's got me tickled. "Not much to tell in that category, but if

I looked like you, had that figure, I'd…" I pause to tease her a bit. "I'd be a whore. I'd show that body to everyone." She likes that sex story.

My other friend is living with a great guy for over 10 years. She's an artist and an antique dealer, paints incredible images on old pieces of furniture. We carry on about the world of men and she gets it. She's a better date than any guy I've met yet. Small, petite, whitish blond hair, she can kick ass and take names.

My birthday, that dreaded 60th, turned out to be one of the best I've had. Girlfriends. They don't let you down.

I partied all week with the girls, but on my actual birthday another girlfriend took me to dinner. I was touched she left her husband at home to make sure I had fun. The night air was heavenly so we ate on the patio outside. Tiny lights like fireflies sparkled around us. I have to describe her as her sister does, a quote I can't claim for my own but love. *She is so southern gothic she has Spanish moss on her head instead of hair.* "This dinner was so wonderful, if you were a guy we'd have sex tonight." I paid her my highest compliment!

A time of loss has also been a time of beginnings. Old friends and new friends connecting and bringing light into my life. I've reunited with a wonderful friend that was my best friend twenty years ago. We lost touch but are now lunching together again. My husband's cousins are calling turning my quiet evenings into lively ones full of discussions and laughter as we remember my husband and talk about my future.

My dear friends, you are all amazing. You are strong and talented and can do it all. You are constantly learning and expanding your horizons. You care for others and know how to make a sad heart happy again. Yes, you are all women, but for me you are the best girlfriends a gal could have. Shit, I'll even say "yes ma'am" to that!

Ode To Margaritas

I love Margaritas, how about you?

I can only handle one, maybe two

Frozen with salt are simply divine

Tequila, triple sec and a wedge of lime.

My hair of the dog hangover cure.

The Invitation

A *glorious* drive in the corvette on one of the rare occasions I have taken it out put me in one very good mood. I had just been shopping at the thrift store and found the best vintage lace blouse, layered ruffle gold silk skirt and brown suede boots. My holiday outfit just in case I get the perfect invitation. I seem to have all the fun clothes, and nowhere to wear them. But, at the prices at Goodwill on senior day, I can't pass anything up. Besides, if I don't wear it, I'll donate it back. Cheaper than any bad habit such as drinking or smoking. And I'll look smokin' in that little outfit. Just off beat enough to please me.

It is the first week of December and I have decided not to send my usual bevy of holiday greeting cards out. All my friends know what my year has been like and I don't want my signature by itself on a card to be another reminder. But that does not stop me from hoping I will find a friendly greeting during this season of the year.

I pull in the drive and stop to check the day's mail. Today there is one white flat envelope staring back at me from inside my mailbox. I pull it out; hold it for a minute. Addressed just to me. I smile. So much of the mail still comes in my husband's name.

Anxiously I rip it open. The top line starts, *you are invited....*

Someone has invited me to a party. I close my eyes for a second and see myself wearing my new outfit to a lovely gathering. Perhaps I'll have a glass of wine and share small talk with friends. Maybe I'll be kissed under the mistletoe. I am happy someone is inviting me somewhere.

I pull the invitation the rest of the way out and my pleasure takes a 180-degree turn to horror. The funeral home that handled my husband's cremation has invited me to a memorial service; a service for all who have lost loved ones during the year.

"Dear God," I whisper quietly. I drop the invite on the dash of the car and head up to the house.

"You need to go," a friend told me. Of course I had to call several friends as soon as my feet hit the kitchen floor.

"Closure," another reminded me.

"Shit," my best friend said.

"Wanna go?" I ask her. She turns down my invitation.

The question is, *do I want to go*? I shake my head, *no, no, no*. I am just trying to enjoy myself the best I can and get the hell past December. Now this.

I talked to a new friend who's son died the year before. "You need to go," he told me. "Do it for him and do it for yourself. I know. Been there."

"We'll see," is all I can manage to reply.

The day of the service it completely slipped my mind. I had to work at the gift shop and while driving there my cell phone started ringing.

"Hey, are you going? It's tonight you know," my friend with his lost son.

"I'll think about it." I feel funny he has called me. I totally forgot the date, and here was a reminder from someone I liked, but barely knew.

This is how I make my decisions these days. *It's a sign*. The timing of his call seemed so weird to me that I knew I was meant to go.

That night I put on the holiday outfit I'd bought at Goodwill and drove around the block to the funeral home. It was practically in my back yard, so I couldn't use traffic as an excuse to miss the service.

As soon as I sat down and looked around I knew I should not have come. Everyone was old. Old ladies, old men. No one my age. No one to feel that kindred spirit with. No one to share the words, "We're too young to have had this loss." Not even someone's cute son to send a smile in my direction.

Everyone there was so old that it was no surprise they were there. Old people remembering older friends. *Be nice*, I chide myself.

The funeral home chapel reminded me of my early days as a teenager when I went to church with my family. I haven't been in years. I am spiritual, but I don't feel comfort in church. I believe in God, but I believe in helping others rather than sitting in a pew.

The organ played and the sermon began. I started to fill up with tears. *No, not here, not now* I prayed. My thoughts turned to my husband and I almost giggled I was so nervous. He would have a fit I was here. He did not like the formalities of funeral homes or churches and this certainly would have mortified him. I tuned out the sermon and all I could think of was getting pizza on my way home. A diversion from the sounds around me and a yummy one at that.

By the time I headed to the car, all thoughts of pizza left. I had made it through what I considered an ordeal, not a healing moment. The final straw the little red candle in the paper bag they thrust into my hand as I walked out of the chapel.

I'll just go to Kroger and pick up a rotisserie chicken. The memorial service had unnerved me. What was the purpose of my going? *Signs*. Someday maybe I'll rely on common sense and forget to watch for *signs from beyond*.

I pulled into the Kroger parking lot and hopped out of my van. As I locked the door a young woman came up behind me and startled me.

"Can you spare some change?" she asked.

I looked at her under the parking lot lights. She was in her early forties, very clean looking, dressed in jeans and a sweater.

"I live in my car, have no home, no money," she continued.

I knew her. I recognized her. We have had this conversation before. Only it was over a year ago, that spring when my husband first became ill. I was coming home from picking up two rotisserie chickens, a few diet cokes and salad fixings for dinner. I'd forgotten my husband's pack of cigarettes and stopped at the convenience store. The same girl came up to me then saying the same thing. There was something about her that touched me. She looked so nice to be begging for money.

That day I told her, "I don't have cash, but I have two cooked chickens." I know I sounded crazy. "Would you like one?"

"Yes, I haven't eaten in a day." She took me by surprise with her answer.

I pulled out the extra chicken and a canned drink and handed them to her.

"God bless you." She gave me the faintest smile and walked off with her meal. I could see her in the rear mirror as I drove away, eating the chicken.

Now here she is again. After all those months. Talk about déjà vu.

"No money, but I am buying groceries. If you wait, I'll be back with a chicken for you."

She nodded and I took off into Kroger anxious to get some food for her and myself. I came back with my bag of groceries and couldn't find her. As I was looking around the semi-lit lot she appeared behind me again.

"Here." I handed her the food. "Take care of yourself."

She grabbed the sack and headed back to wherever she came from. Before she vanished she turned and called back to me, "God bless you."

I thought about my evening on the drive home. I had convinced myself I had to go to that memorial service because of something to do with me. Maybe it would make me feel better. It certainly didn't. But I knew with my friend's call I had to be there.

Was it possible my invitation was not for a memorial service? But an invitation for dinner? Not to nourish my memories, but to feed a homeless woman whose story I'll never know.

Perhaps I'll still believe in signs to guide me. The nudge to go to the memorial service put me at the right place at the right time to share a moment of grace with a stranger. Who would have thought a rotisserie chicken would ease me into the holiday spirit?

Yes, Barbara,
There Really Is A Santa Claus

Christmas. The holiday I have been dreading is about ready to come down my chimney. Maybe I'll bake some cookies, but hell, I don't cook. Besides, my gas oven could be too tempting to stick my head in if I get any more depressed.

This is my first Christmas without my husband. The hardest, I am told by friends who still have their mates. Just make it through the day and you'll feel better, they reassure me. I feel so bleak not even Santa can cheer me.

"What do you want for Christmas?" one of my girlfriends asked earlier this week.

"I want last Christmas, when I had my husband." Then feeling like a grinch I looked at her and smiled. "OK, maybe I'll write Santa to drop a man in my stocking as he passes by."

"One in your pants might be better," my dear friend touches my arm. "That's my girl, chin up."

That thought alone made me laugh. "Have had enough guys who want in my pants without Santa's help, thank you kindly."

"At least you don't have the cook for ten, can't believe everyone is coming to my house again this year." She winced on that comment.

"My mother-in-law is cooking for the *orphans*. That's what she calls her friends whose children aren't coming for Christmas." I shake my head. "I am so happy she has plans, or I'd worry about her. I'm worried enough about myself this Christmas."

"And you had such fun with your mom's visit last weekend. So that was a good present, right?"

"The best."

Home alone for the holidays. I looked at my little Christmas tree. Pleased I put one up with all my grumbling. All my old ornaments went to my booth at Kudzu Antiques in hopes they would sell. The botanical gardens inspired this year's tree. The nature theme, not how I interpreted it. Artificial, four feet tall, it is full of tiny white lights, frogs, bugs and snakes. A plastic water lily sits proudly on top. *Oh little tree how cute you are.* It makes me laugh to look at it. It also reminds me I need to make some plans for Christmas so I won't end up face down in a pity pie.

"I'm coming for dinner on Christmas day." I called my best friend, the chef. "Please tell me you're not cooking any of that Thai crap." I have a thing about Thai food. How come everyone, but everyone I know loves it? Not me. I am still the burger and fries gal with a touch of Mexicana. I want a man who eats meat, a throwback to cavemen days, not a modern sensitive man who eats Thai.

My last dating profile began with *No Thai Food Please.* Then I declared to the male population, *I have found men who eat Thai, don't like me.* It's the absolute truth. They don't. But just how appealing that makes me on the dating menu I'm not sure. I got only one quick comment on that profile. A man from California wrote to me, *I guess you did your research on that one.*

I was pleased with myself I was going to my best friend's house for Christmas day. *Bring a DVD,* I made a note to myself and stuck it to the fridge door. Then I grabbed a diet coke and a bag of chips and plopped down in front of the computer. A new man had written to me. *I'm in town for the holidays visiting my kids, but have Christmas night free. Want to have a drink and say hello?*

Would love to meet, I immediately replied. Well Santa and his elves were hard at work that's for sure. Already I felt a sprinkle of Christmas magic on the top of my head.

It was hard to find a restaurant on Christmas night, but a small pub in downtown Decatur kept its doors open for the locals. We decided to meet there. He was a very pleasant looking man, mid sixties, a bit on the hefty side. He looked cool in his vintage leather bomber jacket that hid his waistline which I guessed was as charming as my own.

"You look different than your photo, can't figure out why?" I was definitely checking him out. He looked different, but that was not a bad thing.

"It's the goatee," he smiled when he stoked it. "Trying something new. Like it?"

Actually I did. "Santa couldn't have looked better."

"Oh, and that darn photo. My kids put my profile up. Used an old photo."

I had liked the photo of him, tall, thin, standing next to his motorcycle. But I liked this version too.

"Grew up right in this area," he told me over a beer. "Avondale Estates. Still have my mother's old house. Will move back to it when I retire next fall." I watched his face soften as he spoke of his mother. A widower, he had been married to his high school sweetheart until three years ago.

The lights from the pub twinkled around us but were no match for the twinkle in his eyes. My very own Santa stopping on his rounds to entertain me.

I took my last sip of coffee and shivered a little in the night air. He reached over and his hand just briefly touched mine. "Do you like Christmas lights?" he asked me.

"Who doesn't?"

"So let me show you the lights in my neighborhood. The folks there put on quite a display." He pointed to the largest truck I've ever laid eyes on and off we went.

He knew someone in almost every house and remembered the name of every kid who had lived there. I was laughing over tales of his childhood and my widow's heart started to feel full of glee. His town had come alive, with stories spun so sweetly like sugar candy. I gobbled up every word that flew from his mouth.

I was bedazzled by all the lights before me and wondered if I should have brought my cat eye sunshades to protect me from the heavenly glow surrounding me. Candy canes burst through the rooftops and large plastic Santas sparkled on every corner. My face felt frozen in time with the cold night air blowing in the open truck windows while my feet were toasty warm from his heater.

"Ooooh," I sighed spying the tree on the lake. Looking like two trees on top of each other the reflection was so sharp and clear in the dark water. Who knew this fairyland was so close to my home?

"The founder of the Waffle House used to live here," he pointed out his open window to a house that was hidden by trees. "You know the original Waffle House is now a museum about two miles down the road."

Our next stop on the tour of homes was a charming old bungalow that had piles of lumber stacked in the front yard. "That house is being renovated by musicians, some famous group, but I can't remember their names." It didn't matter to me who they were; I just loved his stories.

Finally we reached his old home. "That's the house I grew up in. Mother died a few years back, but I'll be coming back to it."

I was lost in the Christmas wonderland he had provided for me.

His stories so full of sentiment and memories of his joyous youth filled my heart with magic. I had that same feeling I used to get as a child waiting for Santa.

"I'm hungry." I don't know if he said it or I did, but suddenly I was starved.

Visions of waffles danced through my head
With my handsome driver so lively and quick
The Waffle House was the place we had picked
Oh waffles, oh grits, oh coffee and eggs
Soon I was sitting on the stool, dangling my legs

The Waffle House. The hottest place to be at 10PM on Christmas night. Buzzing with activity, the booths were all full. We sat at the counter and felt the steam from the grill tickle our noses. I ordered a meal and snarfed it all down. A final guzzle of coffee and I looked at him. "Did I eat more than you?"

He shook his head and touched his goatee, "Oh, Barbara, I think you did."

His appetite was as big as mine. So we ended our meal with a huge piece of pie. This festive evening gave me apple pie not the pity pie I had fretted over earlier in the week.

He drove me back to my van where we said our *goodbyes*.

But I swear I heard him exclaim as his truck drove out of sight, "Merry Christmas to all, and to all a good night."

First Snow

"*Do you*think it will really snow today?" I ask my girlfriend with the Madonna hair. "Are you OK coming out in this weather?"

We are planning on lunch and antiquing. The weather station is planning on snow. They've been planning on it all week, but so far nothing. The first of February and snow may be in the air.

"Don't be silly, I'm heading over now. I'm from Ohio, we're not afraid of snow there. You are such a sissy."

"Sissy? Get your butt over here. I want to have some fun."

She's right. Everything new that comes my way this year is a hurdle in my mind. I jump over it, but not without first worrying about it. I have my mental checklist. First snow is now on the top. Dreading it.

I remember too many ice storms where the power was out for days. Even an hour without power makes me uneasy. What would I do? My husband was always prepared for weather emergencies. I don't even have back up batteries for the flashlight. Come to think of it, where is that flashlight?

Snow with a husband can be romantic. Power outage can mean sex. *Get real*, I remind myself. I am thinking romantic novel. Power outage to my husband meant getting the firewood in, pulling out the kerosene lanterns and marching around the perimeter of the house checking for damage. I would stay under my quilt reading. But a snow day with a loved one is a cozy time.

I look out the front window just as my friend's car pulls in the drive. Snowflakes have started falling. Big damp flakes that hit your nose and melt.

She was laughing as I ran out to greet her. "Wouldn't you figure the snow would start just as I am getting here?"

"Doesn't look like it will be much." I looked around through the falling snow into the bright sun above.

"Let's go to Moe's." I was in the mood for Mexican food and it was right up the street from the house. I jumped in her car and off we went.

"Glad you are still open," I told the guy fixing our lunch. No one else was in line, so maybe there were other sissies out there afraid of what this weather would bring. Sure glad I wasn't one of them today. "Extra queso and chips, please."

"Have you got time to shop?" I ask my friend. She has a 30 mile drive back to her house and I wasn't sure she should stay but I wasn't ready to head home.

"Looks fine out there. Let's hit a few places then I'll go. This is nothing."

All my favorite places are within a few miles of my house. First we stopped at Decatur Estates where I have my jewelry case. I wanted to see if anything had sold. I hadn't been to check on it in a few days. Selling gives me my excuse to buy. *As if I need an excuse.*

Within walking distance was another favorite place of mine, The Last Chance Thrift Store. They were still open and I found a great quilt for the couch. *The dogs and I can warm up under it tonight* I thought.

"We're closing in thirty," a voice boomed out over the PA system. I looked outside and the snow was starting to stick. I paid for my purchase and we took off.

"Let's go by Kudzu antiques," my friend suggested. "Am looking for some rhinestone necklaces for the clocks I'm decorating.

You don't have any, do you?" I didn't. My jewelry has beetles and frogs on it.

Our last stop was The Bead Shoppe in Avondale Estates. We both needed glue. I discovered this lovely shop and its warm friendly owners when I started making my jewelry. Right next to the Salvation Army store I can't believe it took me months to finally see it. Now I am there a lot.

"We're just closing but come in. You know I can't turn you away." The young owner gave me a quick hug and a big smile.

"Look at that snow, we won't be long." The parking lot was covered in a think white layer. The snow was finally starting to stick.

"Maybe we should go." I looked at my friend, getting a little worried about her drive home. It was only early afternoon, but the weather was changing rapidly from pleasant to possible trouble.

We drove back to my house, her wheels crunching the crisp cold snow below. Our path took us down the side streets where there was little traffic, so the roads were white until we made them ugly with her tires.

"Oh look," I sighed as we drove up to my house. My front lawn was a winter wonderland. Big white fluffy flakes covered every inch of my yard. The tall loblolly pines were speckled in white. This was a gentle soft snow. No ice, no downed lines, just a fairyland of white across the yards and streets.

"Drive carefully." I hugged my friend as she headed back home. The expressway would be clear for her even though the local streets were covered in snow. As I closed the door I rested my head on it.

Damn, I miss him. I remember the photos I took of him eight years ago in a much heavier snow. He was standing outside leaning on a huge pine tree. I snapped it from the front window when he wasn't looking. He had just pulled a huge limb across the yard and was catching his breath. The yard completely white around him. He is wearing his jeans, old and worn, a thick cotton sweatshirt, bandana around his neck, dark navy cap on his head and nubby work gloves on his hands. His thick longer hair has silver highlights under the old cap, and tiny snowflakes like little white flecks shimmer on his mustache. That photo shows how rugged and handsome he was. My very own Paul Bunyan.

I opened the back door and called for Foxy. Jake was sleeping on his mat.

"Come on, girl," I beckoned her. "Let's check the property."

She ran out ahead of me, her small paws leaving prints in the snow as she raced around the back yard. She stopped for a minute, her snoot up in the air sniffing its cold wetness, refreshing after the dry heat in the house. Then she bolted up to the patio ready to head back in.

I linger a moment to take in all the beauty. The snow will be melted shortly, but for now it is thick on the ground. I close the kitchen door and smile thinking about this lovely day with my friend. She has given me new memories of a snow day to place with those old ones of a life so long ago. My thoughts travel back to my husband and my heart is as full of his memory as my yard is full of snowflakes.

Widows and Travel

"Are you going to travel now?" Everyone asks me that question. I guess as a widow travel is expected of me. That somehow packing my bags and going on a trip will cure what ails me. Sitting here wrapped in my quilt looking out at the cold winter day I wonder if maybe they are right. A patch of warm sunshine on my face now would be heaven.

Then Foxy comes up and licks my cheek. "Good girl," I kiss her back. Why would I leave her and Jake to go on a trip? I love being with my dogs in the house. I'd miss them more than the fun I would have.

I call my best friend, the world traveler. "Do you think I'm being wimpy not wanting to head out, travel, hit the road?" I worry maybe I should do this. Have a complete personality change in how I handle things and try something new. But I really don't want too.

"You guys never traveled, only to see both your moms, so why are you asking?" I've confused her with my question.

"Well, even my vet asked me if I was going to take a cruise when Foxy went for her shots last week."

"Do what makes you comfortable and don't worry about what everyone says." I sighed when she said that. Relieved I didn't have to book a flight to some strange land so everyone I know could relax. "She's traveling. She'll be fine."

My husband and I rarely went on vacations. We did travel to see our parents in the van, full of tools, luggage and dogs. We discovered early in our relationship that mothers are about the only people who enjoy seeing you arrive with two large dogs in tow.

I did go to London with my mother after my father died in the late eighties. See, *widow travel.* But my mother always loved to travel so that was natural for her. Lucky for me, I got to go with her. Her love of travel is the only reason I can say I have been out of the country.

It was fall of 1989 when we took off to London. My husband was less than thrilled I would be gone for ten days but understanding of my need to go with my mother. *Phantom Of The Opera* was at the height of its popularity and mother was determined to see it. She tried to buy tickets as soon as we got to London, but they were sold out. Somehow she found a shop in a back alley off of a street in London's West End that had tickets for sale. She marched in with a fist full of dollars and came out with two tickets. To this day I have no idea how much they cost. But knowing my mother no price would have been too high.

A few weeks later back at the office all the girls were huddled around a fellow co-worker who had just visited New York City. They were listening intently as she eagerly talked about seeing *Phantom of the Opera.*

"Absolutely fabulous." She was radiant as she talked about the play. Then she smiled in my direction, grabbed my hand, and said to the group, "Barbara knows, she saw Phantom too."

They turned their attention from her to me. "Did you see Phantom in New York?"

I smiled and said the words that at no other moment could have been so perfectly timed. "No, London."

That trip to London may have provided me with the best comeback ever. For one who rarely traveled it was my moment of fame. I may request it to be my epitaph, *She Saw Phantom In London.*

I did have one strange but lovely flirtation with a man from Pennsylvania during late fall. We never met but he made me think travel with him would be fun. Our paths crossed with the help of another dating service. Over a six-week period we talked endlessly on the phone. His wife had died some years before. We talked about her, we talked about my husband and then we talked about everything we liked. I think what I liked best about him was the life he had with his wife for thirty years.

"Get your passport," he urged me one night on the phone. We had been talking from midnight to 6AM. "I love to travel and if we hit it off, I want you to come with me." He had such wonderful stories of his travels with his wife I wanted to be a part of it too.

"I'm coming to meet you in the next few weeks and then we'll know if there is a *you and me*," he told me on several occasions. "Be ready." His voice held promise. He was in his late fifties, tall, dark hair and from his photos, very handsome. How could I not indulge in this fantasy?

My passport expired ten years ago. It was time to get a new one. I had better be prepared. I grabbed my debit card, birth certificate, expired passport and headed for the post office.

"Can I expedite it?" I asked the woman who handed me the form to complete.

"There's a fee to do that, but yes you can." She looked at me with interest. "Where are you planning on going?"

"Don't have a clue." I felt a little silly saying this to her, but I wanted to have it *just in case*. To me sooner is always better than later. I completed the form, had my photo taken and handed her the cash I'd gotten with my debit card.

That was on Monday. By Friday I had my passport in my mailbox. And three days later my flirtation with the man who urged me to get my passport was over.

"I've got the sniffles." He called at midnight. "I'm in my PJ's and nightcap and am heading to bed." *Whoa.* This was from a man who told me all he wore to bed was a smile. It was hard to imagine him in a wee winkie cap.

I called him the next day and woke him up. "Just worried about you." I felt uneasy with his tone when he answered.

"You'll learn I don't like to be bothered when I am sick." His manner had taken a turn in a direction I did not like. "I'll call you later."

We did talk over the weekend but the excitement of all those late night conversations was replaced with the revelation how quickly his personality could change. He lived I am happy to report, but our budding romance died.

Sometimes I worry I am too complacent. I think I constantly tie myself down with the things I love; my family, my dogs, my house, my simple life. Everyone asking me about travel now has me asking myself that same question. "Should I take a trip?"

"Soon," I tell myself. There will be a day in the not so distant future when I load up the dogs and hit the road. Visit family again. Small steps first. As for my passport, well it is good for the next ten years.

Post-It Notes

They are all over my house. Sticking on the bathroom mirror, hanging on the fridge, stuck to the top of my computer. Post-It Notes in ultra shades of hot pink, aqua, yellow, lavender, and green are everywhere I look. These 3"x 3" colorful squares, reminders of life's lessons learned.

Take a risk and find yourself.

It's fun to kiss a stranger, but always hug a friend.

Hugging cures a social disease, loneliness.

It's fine to slap a bad date, but more fun to kiss a naughty one.

Give a frog a chance. The worst that can happen is you'll have a pet frog.

Keep your knickers on until you are sure.

Without hope I am just a widow on Xanax.

Pizza, could it be the new antidepressant?

It doesn't matter if a dog's breath is bad, you'll kiss him anyway.

No matter what a guy tells you, there is a penis in his pants.

A good man is hard to find, but a great dog can be found at the shelter around the corner.

At the end of the day it is better to be sleeping with dogs than a dog of a date.

Chill

Spring Back

Whenever I feel blue,
I start breathing again.

Buying Grass Seed

Can tears make grass seed grow? There I was in Home Depot's gardening center, looking at bags of seed and I started crying. There is a water shortage, so maybe this is a good thing. *Cry me a lawn.* Perhaps there is a song there if I work on it. For now I quickly brush my eyes with the back of my hand and remind myself, *the Reverend said fifty pounds of seed.*

Spring is just around the corner and the front yard needs to be seeded. Last year at this time my husband was still alive, but he didn't have the strength to seed the yard. He did continue to mow it on his riding lawnmower almost up to the last month of his life. He could sit on the lawnmower and run the controls with out exerting too much energy. Later he would come back into the house, color in his cheeks, sweating and grinning from enjoying the outdoors. He could hardly walk but he could ride that mower.

Now I sit in the living room and watch as the Reverend mows the front lawn, my husband's old riding lawn mower making circles as it covers the ground cutting the grass. The Reverend has been my blessing. Sent from the heavens when my husband was alive, perhaps to be an angel for me after my husband was gone.

In his late sixties, the Reverend is a kindly black man who is the pastor of a church close to my neighborhood. He is a big man, tall, and heavyset. He smiles a friendly smile, missing a tooth in front, wiping sweat off his brow as he talks to me about the yard.

The first time I met the Reverend was during a severe ice storm six years ago. My husband had just had surgery for a detached retina and had to stay immobile. I woke up on Saturday morning to the sound of limbs crashing to the ground from the tall loblolly pines in our yard. I looked at the clock just as the power went out. It was 7 AM.

Shit. I jumped out of bed and raced down the hall to check on my husband who was confined to a chair in the living room.

"You'd better get some firewood," his morning greeting to me. A little chuckle as he said it knowing how I hate to do these things.

By mid morning the yard was covered with limbs and debris from the ice storm. I had hauled in several loads of wood and a nice toasty fire was going to keep us warm.

That afternoon I saw the Reverend working in another yard and ran up to him.

"Can you help?" I anxiously asked. "A large tree fell in the side yard." I had to get that tree out, for my stubborn husband would have disregarded the doctor's orders and tried to do it himself.

"Why yes ma'am, I can," he smiled at me.

He came back the next day with his son and within a few hours the yard had been put back in order, a huge pile of limbs at the street and a nice stack of firewood by the back door.

I would not need the Reverend's services again for some time.

My husband was back up in a few weeks and could be found outside on most days. He would wave to the Reverend when he saw him across the street or stop to chat with him when he parked his van in front of our house.

"Who's going to mow your yard now?" My husband's best friend asked me shortly after my husband died. "It's huge, you can't do." He was right. The yard would be a problem. I was not getting on the riding lawnmower. The slant towards the right of way would be my undoing.

I hung up the phone, looked out the front window and saw the Reverend in my neighbor's yard.

"Yes!" I cheered out loud and did a little dance out the door. I ran over and told him about my husband.

"Can you help?" There I was with that question for him again.

"Mow all the widow's yards here." Then he looked sadly at me. "Sure did like your husband, but God takes care of us." I knew I had found my garden angel.

Sitting drinking coffee one morning earlier this week there was a knock on the door. I opened it to see the Reverend in his overalls standing smiling at me.

"You know it's time to aerate the yard, seed and fertilize it, if you want grass," he informed me. It could have been my husband standing there. The very words he would say at this time of year and then his list of lawn and garden chores would begin.

So there I was in Home Depot with the Reverend's list of things to buy; fifty pounds of grass seed and fertilizer, some lime and garden hoses to replace the ones that had split over the winter. The van was loaded and I headed home, the Reverend aerating the ground while he waited for the seed.

I watch the Reverend as he circles my front yard on the riding mower just like my husband did, and I swear I can see my husband smiling, riding with him. He has that jaunty bandana around his neck and a cap on his head, riding without a care in the soft spring day.

The Exorcism

If you were a movie critic, how would this plot rate? *Movie trailer: The widow is in need of an exorcism. Death must take a holiday after two more die in the wake of her year. A psychological drama staring the widow Barbara, who has lost her husband, his cousin and lastly her large dog. Will she continue to rally or will the demons win?*

I am living a bad movie plot. You know the one, you leave the theater crying, blowing your nose into Kleenex and scaring the hell out of the date who thought you were cute earlier in the evening.

After my husband died his cousin and I became very close. We were kindred spirits and talked until the wee hours of the morning. Easy for her, she lived in California so it was still early on her coast, and easy for me as I stayed up most of the night.

She was a retired VA psychiatric nurse, but was very in tune with the psychic world. We would talk for hours sharing stories, sorting out life's issues and mostly she let me talk about my husband. Many of her friends were in the psychic intuitive community, and she wanted me to speak to one. "It would help you so much with your healing," she would tell me. She ended her calls with the same words, "Get a reading."

She was not the only one suggesting I get in touch with the psychic world. A male friend of mine got readings over the phone on a regular basis. The readings helped him channel his life in the direction he wanted. He was excited when I picked up the phone.

"You came up in the conversation," he informed me. "My

psychic told me you are surrounded by positive energy and will re-marry." *How nice he spent his money to find out my future.* "Call her and get a reading," he urged me.

"Why?" I asked. "You just told me everything I need to know."

I am a believer of sorts. Not the movie type of psychic schlock, where someone predicts the future, the base for a horror story that has you gripping the chair in a nervous frenzy. I believe in psychic energy and that the universe will give you what you need if you are open to it. For those professionals in the intuitive field, please excuse my lack of knowledge, but my heart is in the right place.

I like to pick and choose which information from the psychic community to act on. I remember the day my husband's cousin called me worried about my finances.

"Your IRA is in trouble," she informed me. "You need to have cash on hand, not in the stock market."

That got my attention. I don't have a financial background, but it didn't take a rocket scientist to know my IRA was loosing money. Couldn't miss that one. It was on the news every night.

I called my stockbroker the next morning.

"I need to sell some stocks and put the money in my cash account."

He started to protest, but I cut him off mid sentence. "I am getting my information from the psychic world."

"That's what I'm here for, you don't need psychic financial counseling." He was amused with me I could tell. "But let's take a look at what you've got."

He looked at my portfolio. "You do have a few stocks at higher risk, we'll get rid of those."

That night I called my husband's cousin back. "Guess what, I took your advice and sold some stocks." I was quite pleased with myself.

"Nooooo," she had a way of drawing her words out, "I didn't mean now. Mercury is in retrograde and you should have waited."

How was I to know? I'm not a psychic.

My husband's cousin became ill suddenly mid February. One of her friends had a dream that saw her young, smiling in a beautiful house. She was calling and beckoning, "Come for tea." As she climbed the steps to the house, the steps disappeared and there were clouds below. My husband's cousin died shortly after that dream at age 62.

In April my old dog Jake gave up the ghost. That Saturday morning was like any other. He had eaten a hearty bowl of dog food and I had changed his bellyband. The weather was wonderful and I went to visit T, a gal with the best garden junk piled high in her yard. I filled my van with old cracked flowerpots, garden statues and rusty cans full of violas.

I got home late afternoon, unloaded the van and went to check on the dogs. Jake was semi-conscious, his mouth like ice. He was in shock.

I called my neighbor. "Can you help me with Jake? I need to get him in the car and to the vet."

He came right over. "Want me to go with you?"

"No. I'll be OK. Just don't want Jake to linger and suffer. This is it."

My neighbor touched my arm.

"You know I've been worried if his front legs went I couldn't handle him. At least it didn't come to that." We hugged and I drove off.

The vet who had so lovingly given Jake his acupuncture gave him the final shot to ease any pain.

I held his head in my hands, kissing him in that final moment. He was unaware of anything. He had said his *goodbye* and left me to tidy the final details.

That night I had to clear the house of all the things that had made keeping Jake easier. I pulled the tarps from under the rugs, got the heavy mats off the floors and pitched his bellybands and the remaining Kotex pads. I hauled it all to the street at midnight for the garbage men on Monday. Lugging everything down the driveway, sobbing, I chanted to myself, *death is leaving my house, death is leaving my house.* A demented woman on a mission filled with grief. Lucky for me my neighbors were asleep. My head may have been spinning on my shoulders.

The darkness of that night scared me. I cried until I thought my eyes would swell shut and I might never see again. I missed everyone and nothing could comfort me. Exhausted I fell into bed with faithful Foxy lying close to me.

The next morning when I awoke I felt strangely at peace. Jake's death cleared my house of its ghosts. I lived knowing he was dying, I outlived my husband and I lost a best friend. But the sun was bright as I eased out of bed.

I am putting the drama of this year behind me. My heart is full of the memories of those I loved and lost. I still talk to them. I remind my husband he was my handsome leading man in the story of our life. I tell his cousin I am so not getting a reading. I whisper, "Good boy, Jake."

The movie critics have given my story a thumbs up. Their review? This drama has plot turns at every corner. The ending is a mystery. Watch for the sequel to find the answers.

The star of my own romantic comedy, that's how I see my life now. After all, a psychic told me it was so.

I sit outside with Foxy next to me and in the soft rustling of the leaves I swear I hear my husband's cousin saying, "Way to gooooo, girl."

On Bookstores, Lipstick and Men

I love books. I collect books. Sometimes I even read books. My attention span when reading is short, but my affair with books has been long lasting. I tried writing children's stories in my forties. They are tucked in a folder hidden under the bed. Twenty years later I still find delight in entering a bookstore and am trying my hand at writing again.

In the years before I met my husband and before antiques took over my life, I hung around with a literary crowd. My good buddy Cliff owned The Old New York Bookshop in Midtown, an old neighborhood close to downtown Atlanta. Now a stylish renovated neighborhood, back then that area of town was questionable.

His shop was in a Victorian cottage with its lopsided corners and slightly sagging floors. The rambling rooms were filled floor to ceiling with bookshelves. It was a wonder the house held up under the weight of all his books. He sold used and vintage books in the shop and privately sold rare books. Many of his friends are well known authors, but in those early days, at the beginning of their careers, he would throw lavish parties for them. Champagne flowed at the book signings and laughter echoed late into the night air outside.

His shop was on my path home from work. I liked to stop there for coffee during the week.

"So, when is the next party and who is the author?" I asked him as I reached for the coffee mug with my name on it. There was a rack of mugs for the regulars and a constant pot of dark black coffee going. Then I'd flop down on an old comfy chair and shoot the bull with him. By then someone else would come in, join us and grab their cup.

The old house is still standing, but my friend sells privately and online now. He contacted me shortly after my husband died. "Let's meet for lunch."

We had lost touch with each other over the years, so I was anxious to hear about his family. His wife and her friend had written a cookbook *The One Armed-Cook* and I wanted details.

"God you look just the same, how is that possible?" I gave him a big hug. He is a short Jewish guy with a wicked sense of humor and hasn't aged a bit. We caught up on our news then reminisced about the old days.

"I miss your shop and all those parties." The waitress had just handed us the menus. "Hard to top some of those gatherings. And the stories..." I rolled my eyes and laughed.

"Yeah, those were great times. You know, I found the old rack of cups the other day going through boxes in the garage. Your cup was crusted on the bottom. Did you ever wash it?"

I swatted him with the menu. Same old Cliff. Some things never change.

There will never be a bookshop quite like that one for me. But there are bookstores I love today. So I don't have my mug on the wall, but I can visit a bookshop that sells coffee and get a steaming hot cup to enjoy while I flip through the latest books.

No date on Saturday night? Not a problem. I like to head to Barnes & Noble, grab a book, look for the most interesting man reading and sit down next to him. Never mind we don't speak we are sharing the same experience.

Thanks to an online dating service I found a wonderful

independent bookstore close to my home, Eagle Eye Bookshop in Decatur. A romance was rekindled there that may last a lifetime. My love of writing has met its muse. In the back of this charming shop, full of used and new books, I found a class on screenplay writing and a teacher who has inspired me to write into the wee morning hours. I met a new man for a date and signed up for a writing class. Not the typical expectation from online dating, but typical for me. I can't seem to get a second date, but those first dates bring me something better.

Let's meet for coffee, his e-mail began. *I am taking a screenplay class down the street from you, we'll meet afterwards.* I looked at his profile and a friendly smile looked back at me.

Tell me about the class. I wrote back immediately. *Do you think I can sit in on it? I'm trying to write and need help.* I had started a journal on my widow thoughts, trying to capture my wacky, emotional life since my husband's death.

An hour later I got his reply. *Teacher says you can join us tonight. Be there a little before class so you can meet him.* The rest of his e-mail telling me we'll go out afterwards fades to black.

One of the few times I was early. But the rain and traffic made everyone else late. By the time the class started I was feeling a buzz of excitement and a little nervous. My date had not arrived yet.

The class had six students, all with writing backgrounds. The teacher made me smile as soon as I saw him. An Englishman in his mid forties. He was dressed in a black t-shirt, jeans with a cap on his head. His ease at teaching and his charm filled the room with warmth. I loved his British accent. His background was of the horror / zombie genre, which added a bit of spice to the class for me, the gal writing the widow journal.

My date finally arrived and sat down next to me. He was in his

early sixties, slightly graying hair wind blown from the storm outside. He turned to me with an impish smile and whispered, "You're
pretty."

"Shhh," I put my finger to my lips to quiet him. But then I smiled
and whispered back, "Thanks." After all the man just told me I
looked pretty. Can't ignore that.

I signed up for the remaining classes before I left that night. This
was a match that would last. The men might come and go, but writing was a love that would endure. The teacher that night opened up
a door for me that I only dared to peek through earlier in my life.

My date and I headed off to find a glass of wine rather than coffee. I was in a mood to celebrate. He flung his arm around my shoulders like we had done this before as we headed to his car.

He told me what had gotten him interested in writing and we had
a very pleasant conversation. The soft glow of the lights in the café
and a little bit of wine had us laughing and being silly.

"You know what I like on girls?" His eyes twinkled. "Gloss, lip
gloss. And one with flavor."

"Well, I just use lipstick, and when it wears off that's it. Don't
like doing touch-ups in public."

"No, no," he corrected me. "Guys like to see a female putting
on lipstick."

"Seriously?" I am not sure if this is his opinion or some male
information I have become privy too.

"Hmm, I'll have to give it a try and report back to you next
class." It is silly, but I mentally put it on my to do list.

Lipstick from the tube, or perhaps lip gloss with a finger gently
caressing my lips after my next dinner with friends. *Which will it
be*? Whichever I decide to do, I will do it with a flourish as though
I am center stage.

"You watch," he says, " a girl putting on war paint takes the attention." With that he gives me a quick peck, a hug goodnight and drives off into the night.

I can hardly wait for the next class. My real match that night, a writing class. My date, a friend who continues to sit next to me while the teacher has me captivated. But my date triggered my curiosity about lip gloss that night. You can bet next week I will be sitting taking my notes, smiling in his direction with lips that have the faintest shimmer. My only question is *what flavor will I be?*

The BS Artist

Some days when I hear myself talk to others I think, *God Barbara, you are so full of shit.* The bravado with the words that spill out of my mouth astonishes even me. In my new role as *the widow* I am giving advice on relationships, talking about finding my new role in life, and telling stories about strange dates I have had. I tire myself out trying to explain myself.

So I resort to my old ways. I am a storyteller. I like to make people laugh. I can take the smallest incident and escalate it to a rip-roaring tale. Then give me a Margarita, and I may make you blush.

"You are so funny," my friends tell me. "How do you do it?" They like my warped sense of humor.

How can I not do it, I think to myself. I make fun of everything, always have. Humor has saved my life when I thought my life would end.

"Where do you think I'll be in a few years?" I ask those closest to me.

"Just get through the day, the week. Stop worrying," an old friend's advice.

"Maybe I need a plan," I told my best friend.

"Why? You never had one when you were married."

She's right. I never had a plan. I had a husband. For some reason a plan didn't seem to matter. Now it does. How can I be alone and not have some goal, a plan, in mind?

So my plan, I tell those around me, "I am going to write a book."

"Oh you should," they reply. "God those men you meet, those stories. You crack us up."

My friends always say this to me. They think writing a book is something I can do and need to get started on.

"Lots of sex in it," a married friend tells me. "I need a fix. My sex life stinks."

"Well, mine is not much better, but I'll work on something just for you."

"How about two girls together?" Her husband has overheard us from the next room and added his two cents worth.

"It's my widow story," I yell back to him. "Haven't gone there yet, but give me a few more bad dates." My friend covers her mouth like she is gagging. Not at me, at her husband.

My mind is spinning with fragmented thoughts of my first year alone. The lows, the highs, the things I never thought I'd be doing again. How to put them on paper so someone will understand the oddity of it all.

I think of my life before my husband and my story begins.

Many years ago there was a young woman in her early thirties who lived in an inner city neighborhood of Atlanta. She bought an old bungalow that never got renovated. She planted an herb border were Rosemary grew five feet tall. She drove a yellow VW bug that took her on great adventures to other states. She danced the night away with her friends dressed in vintage forties cocktail dresses. She kissed the boys and made them cry.

Her dear friend had a huge Victorian mansion that was in disrepair. Money that should have been spent on the house was spent on glorious parties. Music and laughter filled the air into the wee hours of the morning when her friend entertained. Many of the guests were artists and writers. This young woman standing at her friend's parties was in awe of the talent around her. Her own attempts at children's stories were unfulfilled. She never talked about wanting to write herself, because she was overshadowed by the greatness of others. Time passed and as it sometimes happens, these friends all went their separate ways.

Cut to current day. Now a widow, this woman has reconnected with her good friend who used to give these fabulous parties. One was in full swing when she arrived in the late evening. She could hear the mellow sound of singing as music floated from the house into the night air.

She was a little nervous to be in a crowd where once she knew everyone and now she knew only a few.

"So good to see you," an old friend came up behind her with a hug. "The wine is in the kitchen, grab a glass, hon." Then she took off as quickly as she appeared. The widow was left standing alone.

Two glasses of wine later the widow was feeling very social indeed. She walked up to a couple she had not seen in many years and they started talking.

"We are so sorry to hear about your husband," they shook their heads in unison as they spoke. "What are you doing now?" they asked, waiting to hear a sad story.

"Writing a book." The widow surprised them with her reply. "Yes, I am writing a book." She smiled at them with the smile of one who was going to accomplish something great.

"Have you written before?" the husband, an artist, asked her.

"I had that newsletter for thirteen years," she reminded them. "So yes."

"Of course," they answered nodding together. "How did we forget? You must tell us about your book."

The widow smiled at them. "It all began last May…"

Well as you know, that widow is me and the story is true, almost.

At my last writing class the teacher reminded us, "Writers write, those who talk about writing to others rarely do it."

I laughed and told him about my party conversation. I am writing, every night finds me at the computer until my eyes are crossing. But every so often standing alone at a party with a drink in your hand a bit of BS can make you feel grand.

The Midnight Walk
(My Homage To My Writing Class)

The dogs were the first to notice the strangeness in the cool evening air. Their noses pointed straight up and they sniffed feverously at the dark sky. The crescent moon left odd patches of light on the grass and the soft glow from the side porch was barely noticeable. Tall trees blocked the view of the house, which gave a feeling of isolation. The yard seemed different tonight with shadows deeper than previous nights. The only thing that seemed familiar to her was the strong fragrance of Jasmine floating up from the creek at the end of the property.

It was past midnight when she took the dogs out for their final walk. But that was not an unusual hour for her to be out with them. She shivered ever so slightly not knowing if she was chilled from the night air or if something else made her skin prickle. There was a stillness tonight that made her uneasy. She wished she had worn a sweater over her thin blouse or at least had not taken off her bra earlier when she had changed into her jeans. Somehow she felt vulnerable outside this evening.

The dogs kept straining on their leashes and pulling towards the creek. *OK,* she thought, *let's see what has you both so excited.* They made it as far as the Crepe Myrtle tree on the far side yard when the dogs dropped submissively to the ground. She looked down at their furry bodies cowering against the damp earth. "Well I see I have great protection with you guys," she quietly spoke to them. She shook her head confused by their behavior. There was a rustling in the shrubs and an icy coldness jolted her body. *Oh God, something is out there.*

She trembled knowing there was no longer anyone in the house who could help her. She had always been the one to take the dogs for their late night walk, but when her husband was alive he listened for her return. If she were gone too long he would come looking for her. Now she lived in the house by herself and her imagination played tricks on her sometimes late at night. *Shit, what is it with these damn dogs?* She tried not to think of the noise.

"Come on, guys," she whispered to them and tugged on the leashes. The dogs would not move. "Gotta go, now." This time her voice was stern. She bent down to give a little shove to the larger dog. But both dogs ignored her commands and sniffed at the damp grass. They picked up a scent of something they did not like. The hackles went up on the back of her German Shepherd and her new rescue dog just sat staring out across the yard. She looked around helplessly, but the yard was deep and dark and her closet neighbor was separated from her by the high stone wall on the patio. If she yelled no one would hear her.

This is silly she thought. *Probably an opossum or some other critter.* She held the leashes tight with one hand and reached for her neck with her other hand to swipe at a mosquito. The warmth of her hand touching her neck brought back memories of her husband's caresses. She loved to have her neck rubbed. Standing in the dark she allowed her hand to run gently across her neck and reached inside her blouse just touching the top of each breast.

The snapping of branches brought her back to reality. With both hands she jerked hard on the leashes. "Come!" She tried to turn them back to the house but the dogs pulled forward. Afraid she might lose the dogs in the darkness she held tight and moved closer to the creek with them.

In the moonlight she could see a large form rising out of the water. Now she knew what the dogs had smelled. The fragrant aroma of Jasmine was replaced by a foul pungent odor. Fear had her glued in place. The dogs started barking in unison and jumping at the figure coming towards them. The odor was so putrid she started choking trying not to be sick. Her left hand covered her mouth and nose to help block the stench. Her right hand held the dogs' leashes for dear life.

The form was that of a man, she could tell by the outline of his figure. His height eluded her. He was hunched over and his arms hung loosely by his side. He rambled towards her with an oddly crooked gait. What was left of his clothes was covered in a dark red substance and mud caked on his skin. As he moved closer the moonlight streaming through the tall pines revealed his face. His eyes had rolled back into his head leaving empty sockets. His flesh was decaying and huge open wounds covered his face and arms, the arms he pointed towards her.

The dogs stopped barking as he came closer. *Dear God in heaven, what the hell?* She had no idea what or who was standing in front of her. This half human figure had a gentleness about him as his head turned in her direction. An odd fascination crept through her body. Other than the sick feeling in her gut from the revolting smell coming from him she was no longer afraid. He tried to speak but his voice was garbled and only a low moan came from his rotting throat. A hand reached for her, the fingers stubs of raw flesh. She was surprised when his cold bloody hand touched her arm that she felt a warmth rush through her. She looked at the remains of his face and wondered what he had looked like before.

Shit, I must be crazy she thought, *but it's been a long time between dates.* Most of the men she had met on the dating services had been monsters of some kind. Hardly a good one in the bunch.

How bad could this guy be? She wondered.

Smiling coyly in his direction she reached out to touch his decomposing hand. Her voice got bolder as she looked at him and spoke, asking that question that is all too familiar to singles all over the planet.

"So what are you doing Saturday night?"

Mirror, Mirror On The Wall, Who The Hell Is That?

Ouch! Decided to take a good look at myself in the mirror. Have avoided it for a while, but decided I wanted to see how I looked these days. Now that one hurts. "*On the twelfth month of widowhood my figure said to me: Pizza, Gyros, Quesadillas, Nachos, Burgers, Fries, Onion Rings, Dip, Chips, Rice Pudding, Cheesecake and a Margarita in a salted glass, did not agree with me.*" I've put on some weight. Too many dinners out with friends and too much take-out to bring home. It all adds up.

I am standing before the mirrored doors my husband installed on the closet some twenty years ago. "Will make the room look larger and brighten it up," he told me.

He was right. The mirrors make the room glow and the sun is exposing every inch of my body today. I feel like I have an aura around me as the sunlight cascades in the window behind me bouncing off the mirror in front of me. I feel dizzy looking at myself. And horrified.

I am wearing my favorite underwear, a pink low cut lace bra and French cut cotton briefs. I can see plenty without totally stripping down. I am here to see how I look, not auditioning for a porn file. *I wonder if I could audition?* I laugh at that one. *Get Real.* Hell I rarely strip down. I don't like to run around naked. I scare myself.

"What are you doing?" My husband would ask me after sex as I jumped up to reach for the dresser top. The lights and his glasses off I was safe making that quick run.

"Getting my panties. You know I can't sleep without them." My hand grips the rolled up ball and I flip back on the bed pulling the undies over my legs.

"How could I forget? But you look cute in them."

See you can still be a sex goddess in your knickers.

I've never been a thong gal, even when I was younger and thinner. I like my cotton briefs, not bikinis and not full panties. Low riding on waist and high riding on hips. Not exactly Victoria's Secret material but my favorite under garments. Never have had a complaint about them either. They slip off easily when needed and have enough weight to toss across the room to the dresser out of reach of the dogs.

Try to pitch a thong, bet it stops mid air and drops to the floor like a feather. You could be in danger of slipping on it if you had to make a mad dash for a quick tinkle in the bathroom. *Now how sexy would that be?*

One of my favorite ads on TV is the one for Playtex Bras for the full figure gal. Well, that's me. Full figure plus a little, and of course, a little older than the girls in the ad. But they are me, or I am them, sassy and loving my bra.

My bra is overflowing so I finally have the cleavage I wanted as a young woman. *Did you ever stuff your bra as a kid to make your chest bigger?* I did. Now I don't have to. But wouldn't you know, now I have to wear a bra when it has become fashionable for the younger gals to go without one. The irony of it all.

My thighs are a little too heavy. I mentioned this to my mother the other day and her reply confused me.

"A little too heavy, now don't lie, honey."

"Yeah, maybe I'm being too hard on myself." I thought I was following her lead.

"No sweetie, you are making yourself sound too thin." She shook her head. "Time to diet. I'm only telling you this since I love you and worry."

"Shit." I was a little stunned. *Remind me not to talk about my butt.*

I smiled and hugged my mother. I asked for it. The mirror and my mother told me all I need to know.

It's time. But I knew that before looking. I could feel the extra pounds in places I didn't like. I've finally finished what I call my widow's work, getting everything in order that needed to be done, those things you have to do to make it your own life again. Been there, done it, got a T-shirt. It is size extra-large.

A widow at sixty trying to date again is scary no matter what you weigh. Try dating thin short men after you were used to a very well proportioned man of 6'7" with 270 pounds of muscle. I don't know if those smaller guys have their complaints about me, but I sure do miss a big hunk of a man that made me feel petite no matter what.

I was used to hugging a man and having my face land in his chest. Now when I hug men we knock foreheads or worse yet, their heads are in my chest. At least they have a soft landing spot.

I have put together a few reminders for myself so I don't fall into that trap of saying, *if only I loose a few pounds* to keep me from doing things now.

*I want to look my best, but I don't want to dwell on it.

*Tons of vintage turquoise jewelry takes the eye wherever you place the turquoise.

*A few extra pounds on the hips, keeps wrinkles from my face.

*Confidence turns heads. Fake it if needed. (Can you fake an orgasm? You're home free. But ditch the guy who can't get you there.)

*Leaving your sweater on when your panties and bra come off brings back that old school girl naughty moment. It is also a great a great cure all for sex after a dinner that leaves you feeling too full.

*A low cut top will draw attention to a positive detail.

*Skill conquers all.

*I may not be the only nervous one. There are two of us taking off our clothes.

I love projects. Now I've got one. Healthy eating. I'll figure it out. In the meantime, I've got places to go.

Almost seven. I've got a date. And he's young and thin.

My jeans fit my butt well, tuck it in a bit. My black blouse cut low and tempting.

I've heard that sex is great exercise. Maybe I should start my healthy lifestyle this evening.

I open the door and say, "Hello." Giving my brightest smile I let my hand gently touch my neckline.

"Hey, you look hot in that blouse."

See what I mean? *Enjoy.*

Colonoscopy Caprice

Oh hell, sooner or later you have to have one. I opted for much later and here it is, my *later* staring me in the face. Or should I say 64 ounces of Gatorade looking pretty grim to me. My day of reckoning. *The Colonoscopy Prep.*

Why not talk about it I ask myself? Hell, Katie Couric had hers on TV. Nothing to feel badly about. It is a test everyone should have and it could save a life, yours or mine. There is power in taking control of your health.

The day has been good. I don't have any guilt I should be doing something more with my time. I am doing exactly as told and enjoying having so little responsibility. I had time to myself, played on the computer and Foxy kept me company. She loves it when I stay home all day.

"Lets go poop." The call I always give dogs when it's time to go out. Foxy races for the back door and looks around. Ha! That call was for me. I'm gone. But I love to get her riled up. Next time I'll let her out.

I feel giddy. Perhaps not eating all day puts you in a state of euphoria. I am having food fantasies. Visions of burgers, fries, nachos, pizza and gyros are swimming in my brain. What will I eat tomorrow when my test is done? It is the most important decision on my mind today. Hell with the diet.

Thank heavens my appointment is at 9AM. My neighbor is driving me over and my best friend picking me up. I hope I am not too bitchy when he knocks on my door. I don't know how to start the day without my coffee and I am not allowed even a sip of water. But I'll brush my teeth careful not to swallow the tiniest drop and greet him with a big smile.

"Having a little test on Tuesday." I called him on the phone earlier in the week. "Can't drive and need a ride." He has always been the best neighbor. At age 70 he has the mindset of don't ask, don't tell.

"Glad to help," he replies. No questions to answer, except, "What time you want me there?"

He and my husband were friends. *Over the fence type of friends.* Kind of like Wilson, the neighbor in the old Tim Allen TV show *Home Improvement.*

A huge old stone wall separates our houses. I can just see the top of his head when he is out in his back yard. When my husband was alive if I saw a patch of silver grey bobbing on top of the wall I'd call to my husband in the sunroom. "Neighbor alert." My husband would stop whatever he was doing and pop out the kitchen door to the patio.

"Morning," he'd call across the wall. "Catch today's weather?" They always enjoyed their ritual of talking weather and politics. I often wonder if my neighbor questioned the timing of those visits.

Now I find myself heading out that side door these days if I catch a peek of him. "Morning." I give him my cheery greeting and we talk about the dogs. I think morning chats with my neighbor is a tradition that deserves to be continued.

My prep, starting to drink all those fluids, began at 2PM. I needed a distraction so I joined Facebook. I added twelve friends to my Facebook page today between slugs of fluids.

I should have had this test earlier. My doctor put me on notice, "It's time." I was in for my annual checkup, almost a year since my husband's death. They knew my husband well. My doctor was his doctor for years before he met me. We talked about my husband.

"You know, he had his colonoscopy scheduled and died two weeks before his appointment," I joked with them. "What timing on his part."

They know my sense of humor by now and smiled remembering the big guy who used to come in. The nurses all flirted with him. He was a flirtable guy.

I had a flirt of my own today. A young married male friend I adore called me. I was on my third glass of the infamous Gatorade concoction. Different doctors have you drink different things. Mine had me take a powered jar of something I refuse to remember and mix it with Gatorade. Yummy.

The phone rang and there was his voice that I like so well.

"How you doing, sexy?" he asked.

I smiled and took a big gulp of fluid. "Just fine, playing on Facebook."

"Facebook? You're on Facebook? Hell, I'm not." He laughs that nice laugh of his.

"You're looking pretty good." He was on his computer when he called me from his office and clicked on to see my profile photo.

I down another huge sip. I feel like I will explode if I take in much more fluid.

"Well, you can only see that photo unless you join and become my Facebook friend. Get with the times." I love to tease him.

"Well, I like what I can see in that photo." He is such a flirt.

My day is made. My friend is 46. I am 60. Prepping for the test they give those older folks. But I am on Facebook and he is not. *How cool is that?* Of course, I'll go to my grave before I tell him what I am doing.

I refer to this week as my colonoscopy vacation to my girlfriends. Because girlfriends talk I'm not shy about it with them. The dates just fell in place to give me four days off in a row from my part time job. A mini vacation. How lucky am I?

My fears for today were silly. You hear terrible tales about getting ready the day before. My only issue was drinking all that fluid. It tasted pleasant enough so I can't complain there.

My mother got me through the last 32 ounces. I called her as I was facing the final bottle.

"Talk to me, don't get off the phone until I finish drinking this," I pleaded.

So she chatted away, and I kept taking sips of Gatorade while listening to her. We laughed and had a great time. It was so social, talking and drinking. I pretended I was enjoying happy hour at a local pub.

I've decided, if they could just find a way to let you add a little tequila to the lemon/lime Gatorade prep mixture, I could have enjoyed Margaritas on my colonoscopy holiday. Now that would be a prep worth looking forward too.

Oh God, Oh God, Oh God

Dear God,

I'm worried. Please don't let me grow old alone. I spend my nights talking to my dog and while I am lavished with kisses, she doesn't hold up her end of the conversation.

Sometimes I think I am not interesting enough to keep myself company. But then I haven't met anyone else who is interesting enough either. Why is that?

On the other hand, I don't want an old man I have to care for. One who has to go to bed early and wants me to fix dinner and do his laundry. No God, not that.

Maybe it's this spring weather making me antsy, tickling my hormones a bit with its teasing breeze. Making me ask more questions than normal.

I'll just chill a bit, that's it. There is plenty of time for you to send me my answers. I am assuming you are updating my life plan as I write this. God, is that a yes I hear?

I almost forgot, Margaritas with the girls tonight. How fun. If I want to complain, I'll complain to them. We'll have our girls' pity party and everyone can vent. You have enough to do without listening to me whine.

Until our next chat,
The chillin' widow Barbara

Menu For The Perfect Pity
Party With The Girls

There is nothing more fun than a group of your best gal pals sitting around bitching about life. Mexican food and Margaritas can bring out the best of stories so I am sharing my favorite menu with you.

Large Pitcher Of Frozen Margaritas,
Glasses With Salt On The Rim
Queso Dip
Chips And Salsa
A Second Large Pitcher of Frozen Margaritas,
Fresh Glasses With Salt On The Rim
Enchiladas, Quesadillas, Guacamole Salad
Side Taco
Side Of Black Beans (Going Home Alone So What If I Toot?)
Third Large Pitcher of Margaritas,
Who Cares If They Are Frozen And Just Fill My Old Glass,
Hell With The Salt
Flan, Maybe Two Helpings
Screw The Calories, There's No One Else To Screw

The Grande Dame Of Dogs
grande dame (gränd däm) a woman, esp. an older one, of great dignity or prestige

"Look at that face," the guy next to me at the vets was checking out my dog. Foxy was in for her first visit. She was seven weeks old, just a small puppy. She had all the markings of a German Shepherd except for a black mask that covered her eyes. That mask gave her an expression that drew attention.

Today, thirteen years later, Foxy is still by my side. She and I are the original two in this household. We've been through it all and are here to talk about it. The Grande Dame of dogs, it's her attitude that lets you know she is queen of the house.

Foxy had some big paws to fill. Coming to us the month after Boy died. A little blessing that saved Christmas and put laughter back in this household. It was like a tomb here without Boy. No dog to pet and sadness thick in the air.

My husband was making me depressed watching him grieve.

"Let's get another dog," I suggested every other day.

But he spent his time compiling photos of Boy and sending them to dog breeders of dogs that looked similar to Boy. Boy was a mixed breed, but my husband hoped to find his origins and then a similar dog. We went to Husky rescue, Malamute rescue and the answer was always the same. No one could figure out what Boy was.

"That's it," I snapped one night. *Enough of this BS*. I told myself. "We need another dog." I said it out loud so I would know I meant it.

It was early December, only a month since Boy had died. But it was time. I checked the newspapers at work the next day and found an ad that excited me. *For sale: German Shepherd/Malamute mix puppies 7 weeks old.* As luck had it the owner lived a few miles up the road from our house.

I anxiously picked up the phone and called the number. A woman answered. "Those are my husband's dogs. Got one female left. I think she's promised. Call back at 7 if you want to ask him."

After dinner I called the man and he said we could come look at the dog. I had to drag my husband out the door.

"Not interested," he said, but still allowed me to tug him along. It was getting dark as we drove out and I worried we'd be too late.

"He said she was a cross between an 85 pound Shepherd and a 90 pound Malamute." I tried to get my husband excited. "Bet she'll be a big dog." Silence filled the air.

When we pulled up in front of the house there was a couple in the carport already looking at the puppy. We could see them clearly under the lights and watched for a minute. Suddenly the man holding the puppy came walking up the drive to us. His pace was quick and the pup's legs were dangling as he held her out towards us.

"They can't make up their mind." He sounded disgusted. "If you want her give me seventy dollars and you can have her."

He put her in the right arms, my husband's. A tiny puppy that curled up next to his big chest. I watched as he looked at her with an odd expression.

"What do you think?" I cautiously asked. I didn't want to appear too excited and nix the deal.

"Do what you want."

Did I really hear him say that?

Yes I did. I dished out seventy dollars. I had cashed a check earlier just in case. I paid the man, grabbed the pup from my husband and jumped into the van.

That was the only time I ever heard those words from my husband. I knew this was our dog. He wouldn't admit he wanted her. But he did.

"Go," I yelled at him. I was fearful the other couple would come running up to grab her back. Or worse yet, my husband would change his mind.

It was not a smooth transition. The puppy loved me but was terrified of the tall man with the big voice. Foxy learned the commands *sit* and *stay* immediately. My husband would take her out to the yard and use the same training techniques on her that he had with Boy. She was smart and obedient, but as soon as they came back inside she would run and hide behind me.

Foxy wanted no part of my husband. I was a wreck. Bad enough he was grieving so deeply for Boy, now he had a puppy rejecting him.

It took two months, but Foxy finally bonded with my husband. Out of the blue she trotted into the sunroom while my husband was on the computer. Standing on her hind legs, front paws on the back of his chair, she leaned over and kissed his ears with tiny licks.

"It gave me a little chill, that tiny kiss," he came in grinning.

From that moment on she was his girl and I could breath a sigh of relief that our household was complete again.

The next month her black mask started to fade and she looked like a small German Shepherd with all her other markings. Her personality is that of a Malamute, gregarious and outgoing. Her size mystifies, she peaked at 55 pounds.

"Do you think she'll get any bigger?" my husband kept asking.

One look at her tiny paws and spindly legs and you knew the

answer to that one. I wonder if that dog owner thirteen years ago was a bit of a yarn spinner about the size of her parents.

I look at Foxy and think of all the history we share. From that tiny bundle of a pup that was to be a huge dog, she matured to a medium size dog with a huge personality. She is not a lap dog, but she is a watcher. She kept an eye on my husband in the years I worked and it was the two of them at home. She looked after Jake and initiated him as to who was boss in this house when he arrived. She sat and kept vigil on both when they were sick. Now she follows me from room to room as I move about the house. I can tell she is tired some nights, but she stays close to my side as I stay up way too late. She is an earth mother who never had pups, but mothers those she loves.

Foxy, the dog that has shared my joys and losses. The dog whose job it is to run the house and train all who enter its doors. At thirteen she is truly the Grande Dame of dogs.

Reflections On Men And Dogs

Truth is I have had better luck finding a dog online than a man. That is where I found my new dog, online at an animal rescue shelter in the late night hours. I was just about to check the new list of matches that had been sent to me, when I remembered talking about rescue dogs with a customer at the shop earlier in the day. Shit. I was tired looking at the same old faces on the dating sites and never finding anyone interesting. I decided it would be fun to look at dogs. *Real dogs*, not the human kind I've been matched with.

So many dogs, so little men. Here for my viewing was a plethora of appealing faces with four legs instead of two. *This will be fun,* I thought. I wasn't in the market for another dog just yet. *Soon, maybe.* Jake had only been gone two weeks. *How could it hurt to look?* A phrase that is always the beginning of trouble for me.

Then I found him. A black afghan mix, male, three years old and small at forty pounds. Immediately I wrote to the rescue site, *tell me about him.* I have found that animal shelters reply much quicker to e-mails then men do. By the next day I had all the information on Bray and a meeting was set up at the park. If only I could get a date that quickly or find one that cute.

Morning came early, as it does when you don't go to bed until 4AM. Foxy and I headed for our rendezvous to meet Bray. Foxy was panting with excitement on the seat next to mine. The side window was partially open and she had her nose pointed up sniffing the air as the breeze caught her attention. She had no idea where we were going, but being a dog, she was just happy to be in the car.

Me? I was getting terrified. *Oh God, what am I doing?* I have no experience training a dog. That fell under my husband's skills. *Would two dogs now kill a dating life that had barely started? Am I making a mistake?* I almost called on my cell to turn back. But that would be as bad as the men I complain about having no backbone to meet.

I parked the van and looked at Foxy. "Ok, babe, let's go." I leashed her up and we walked down to the park to meet our fate. In the distance I could see a few dogs and wondered which was our date for the afternoon.

"Barbara and Foxy meet Bray," the charming young girl greeted us. "I think he will be perfect for you both."

I looked at the sweet shy face before me and my heart melted. He had long silky waving black hair, long black ears with a few punk spikes at top and tiny brown eyes. He passed Foxy's butt sniff test immediately.

"He is a shy boy," she told me. "Needs the company of another dog or he gets so nervous he gets sick."

She had been his foster mom for a month and he did well with her house full of dogs and cats. So he most likely would do well with Foxy. One glance at Foxy convinced me. She had that silly smile a dog gets when it is happy. I decided to take a chance on love.

"When can you bring him and what papers do I sign?" We made the arrangements for the following day.

Bray is so skittish. He was feral when found and spent a year in a shelter being socialized. Our first night together I held his face in my hands, those tiny brown nervous eyes watching me from a face black as night. It was the last time he let me touch him for awhile.

"Be who you are, Bray," I whispered to him. I am convinced that dogs understand me. I never get a reply, but this does not shake my belief they have heard me.

Apparently Bray did understand me. For in the hours I am away from the house, Bray is *who he is.* Shy and timid when I am home, his personality livens up when I am gone. Playful? Maybe. Nervous? Could be. Trouble? Yes.

First it was the windowsill. I noticed chips of paint on the hardwood floor.

Hmmm. I was confused. *I wonder where these came from?* It took me two days to look from the floor to the sill on the picture window in the living room. *Oh, my, he's a chewer.*

A few days later I came home and the edge of my 10 ft X 12 ft living room rug had been munched on. Not badly, but how much rug does a dog have to eat before you consider it badly? Not that it was an expensive rug, an incredible find at the thrift store at $45, but it is a large one to replace.

I looked at my sweet boy. "No." I was pretty firm on that. I was sure he understood and didn't give it another thought.

The next day when I got home a larger edge had been eaten. I stitched the rug and sprayed it with something that is made to repel dogs. Personally I haven't found anything yet that repels dogs, have you? Mine eat poop, so my guess is anything goes.

I dropped a small rubber backed area rug over the spot he was chewing. Bray claimed that small rug as his bed and never chewed what was below it again. Did the spray work? I don't think so. But giving him his own bed did.

Unfortunately, with the rug no longer on his mind, he moved on to something else. Bray chewed his way across a wood ottoman and wood chair. It turned out they were not wood, but fiberboard. *Mmmm.* How tasty that must be to a dog. I pitched both pieces and replaced the chair with a grand old leather club chair I found on

Craig's List for $65. I said a silent prayer as it was delivered. *Please don't let Bray like leather as much as fiberboard.* So far my prayer has been answered.

Bray's fur has taken over my house. He sheds like a torn down pillow tossed in the air, feathers flying in all directions. There are tufts of black fur swirling through my rooms, landing in every corner and covering the light colored rugs with layers of black. I keep in shape vacuuming every day. I lied. I don't vacuum *every* day. But I do have a time keeping up with his fur.

He is still so shy and timid, but works that to his advantage. Bray lays quietly on the floor, looking demure, one front black paw daintily crossed over the other. Any dog lover seeing how timid he is finds this a challenge. For as all dog lovers know, if a dog doesn't come to you, you have failed. It is a bigger blow to your ego than having a date walk out.

The final writing class was held at my house. My test to see how we did with company. Just a small group of four. I wanted them to meet Bray and I wanted to expose him to new people.

Bray has captured their attention. Everyone has forgotten I am here.

"Come on, sweet boy." Bray is keeping his distance. The biggest dog lover is trying to pet him.

"Try a biscuit." I hand a few bones to my friend. "He'll usually come for them." Then I remind him, "Bray doesn't like to be touched."

I can sense this dog lover is feeling rejected by my dog. Bray looks at the bones, gets up and gently nips at the end of one. The reward, a little tongue that just hits the top of my friend's hand and then is gone. Bray retreats to assume his demure pose again.

"If you need help with Bray, call me." The class is over and my friend is heading home. "Maybe I can bring my dog to meet him." He is watching Bray wih loving eyes as he walks out the door.

If only I could work men like Bray does. But I am not so demure.

Bray is the companion I wanted for both Foxy and myself. An online match has finally been made. I've found a male who is a keeper. Bray, my sweet new boy. It is so hard to get near him to pet him, but so easy to love him. Time will bring the rest.

My new dating headline will read, *Threesome Looking For A Fourth*. Let's see if that will generate anything interesting from some of those old dogs when they see my online profile now.

My Love Affair With Turquoise Jewelry

Are those two spirits trying to touch base with me this morning? I feel silly thinking this, but maybe my husband and his cousin are trying to contact me through Ebay.

No, I am not drinking sherry at 9AM. I am sipping coffee as I do every day at this hour. My morning ritual. Plug in the coffee maker, fill my favorite floral mug, bring in the e-mails and check Ebay auctions.

I am always searching for vintage turquoise jewelry on Ebay. I have more pieces than I'll ever wear, but that never stops me. As long as it is vintage, chunky and priced right I have to buy it. The more I layer around my neck and wrists when I get dressed, the happier I am. I have discovered no one ever notices what I am wearing. The only compliment I hear is, "LOVE your jewelry!"

My interest with turquoise jewelry began when I retired from the federal government in 2003. I gave all my work clothes to Goodwill and sold my vintage cameos. Turquoise seemed to go with the new me, the antique dealer dressed in jeans and T-shirts.

An old pawn ring popped up with my search list this morning. The large greenish stone full of dark matrix is mounted in heavy Mexican silver. The seller's description says that turquoise is the stone associated with fifth anniversaries. I didn't know that.

My husband and I were married five years. We lived together almost twenty years before that. We celebrated our fifth anniversary the week before he died.

I hit the buy it now button. The ring is mine. It will be my anniversary gift to myself this year. The sunroom is sparkling with the morning light coming in the two large windows. I smile and look around. Greeted only by the dust floating in the air.

"Hello, honey." I am not distracted from my original thought I am being guided to this jewelry. "Love the ring."

I then Google turquoise to see what else I may have overlooked about my favorite stone.

Turquoise is said to provide strength, protection from harm, psychic sensitivity and connection to the spirit world. If a dear friend gives you this stone it is believed you will be protected from negative energy.

Wow. If that just doesn't sum up his cousin. I look at the thin turquoise bracelet on my arm. It was hers. Sent to me after her death.

She was a believer in spirits and psychic energy. She was the family glue, the one who insisted everyone stay in touch. Many lasting friendships were made when she connected one to another.

I remember the fall after my husband died I got a call from her.

"A friend of mine from Santa Cruz is coming to set up for the show at the Atlanta Apparel Mart and needs some help. Can you call her?" It was more of an order than a question.

"She designs beautiful clothes. You're both so artistic, you'll love each other."

And so it was. I met her friend to help set up the booth and a good friendship was started.

I am a believer in angels. People guided to us at the right time to make transitions easier. Someone who shows up just when life goes amuck. Sometimes life friends are made and sometimes they leave quickly again. The mark they have made, however, is lasting.

My husband's cousin was one of my angels after his death. Her friend from the Mart, once a stranger, now another lifeline for me at at a time of loss when my husband's cousin died. A circle of friendship moving forward embracing you with warmth.

I paid for my new ring with Pay Pal. Not that I need another ring, but this is the piece my husband and his cousin guided me to on Ebay, through all the magic of the universe. You can't say *no* to that.

And for those skeptics who don't believe in signs from the spirit world, but do believe in the power of shopping, just remember, any excuse will do when you find that perfect piece of jewelry that must be yours.

A Senior Moment

"I want to eat at that fish place on the corner," my 44-year-old male friend called to make a date. "I'll come over Wednesday. OK?" He lives in a small town an hour north of Atlanta. A midweek date will be a first with him. When we get together it is usually on Saturday because of the distance. So this is a treat.

I met him online last fall. He was shy at our first hello and I wasn't sure he liked me. I wasn't sure I liked him, but I did think he was pretty cute looking. He had an old vintage car and I had my '79 Corvette so we decided to meet over a Sunday lunch and show off our autos.

"Hard to meet a girl who's into cars," he told me before our lunch date.

Well I love my Corvette, but I am not into cars. He knows that now. We made plans to meet halfway between our towns at a nice restaurant that serves a good variety of food.

I saw his car as soon as I pulled into the lot. I parked next to it and took a deep breath before opening my car door. The weather was chilly and I was wearing jeans and a tan suede jacket I had purchased at the thrift store. I braced myself for yet another bad date, but it was fun to get the Corvette on the road. I hadn't had time to drive it much, always hauling furniture in my van. So this was a welcomed jaunt whatever the final outcome.

He was sitting at the bar when I walked in. Dressed in jeans and a long sleeve shirt I could tell he was lean and muscular. His hair was close cut, almost bald looking with the palest hint of grey. He had a nice face and rosy cheeks from being outdoors.

"Let's move to a booth." He got up with his beer in hand. I noticed his tight butt in his jeans as soon as he got off the barstool.

Oh my, he's young, I thought giggling a bit to myself.

"Order what you want, I'm paying," he smiled a little shyly at me. How nice to have someone offer to pay. I was used to paying my own way on the initial meeting.

Somehow we made it from our first meeting to seeing each other on the occasional Saturday. As far as men go, he has been more of a regular date, even though they are far between, than anyone else I have met. We don't have much in common except our love of dogs, but he is easy to be around.

Nothing is rushed with him. If we eat out he likes to take his time drinking a few beers before ordering.

"If you rush something you like, then it's over," he told me one night. I never thought of it in those terms, but he is right. Such a pleasure after all the coffee speed dates from other men I have met online.

He also does not try to rush you into the bedroom, a trait I found exciting. So different from most of the men I had met. I think I was the one who made the first move in that direction with him.

We had not seen each other for awhile when he called to suggest the Wednesday date. He caught me off guard and I started talking a mile a minute about who knows what. He is quiet and I am never sure what to say to bring him out.

"Slow down," he gently told me. "You always talk so fast, always in a hurry." His next words warmed me. "I like to hear what you say."

Wednesday's weather turned out to be sunny and delightful. I decided to wear my pink T-shirt with my jeans. Since it's just a fast food place, I put a delicate strand of turquoise around my neck rather than the larger turquoise pieces I like. A bit of lip-gloss and a touch of blush gave the natural look I wanted for our casual dinner.

My pink T has a little lower neckline than I usually wear. He likes it when I wear something that exposes a little bit of skin so he can gently caress me while he nuzzles my neck. Thank heavens my neck is not showing my age yet. I do like to feel his hands on my skin.

"I like that on you," he says when he picks me up. "Good color."

He is a guy of few words and all of them are always the right words with me. He kisses me quickly. "Necklace makes you look sexy."

We park the car and walk into the fish place. It has been a long time since I've been in a place like this. Not really like the burger places I go for lunch, but not quite a restaurant either.

His hand has slipped over mine, giving it a little squeeze, as we look at the menu printed on the wall behind the counter.

"What looks good?" he asks me.

You do. I resist the temptation to say it.

It appears he is not the only one who is interested in my order.

The young girl behind the counter loudly calls out to me. "Can I show you our senior menu today, ma'am?" She tries to hand me a printout with the specials on it.

I think I froze on the spot I was standing. Just as I was feeling like a teenager, this teenager reminds me I am a senior citizen. She dared to use the words *senior menu* in front of my young date. Oh God, I think an arrow has pierced my heart.

I muster all my dignity and answer, "No thanks, we aren't sure what we want yet."

But I do know what I want. I want to eat at one of the local pubs or small restaurants that don't offer senior discounts.

Did he hear her asking me that? I wondered for a minute. Then I relaxed. He won't care because age makes no difference to him. We've had that conversation.

I smile sweetly at her. "I'll take the two planks of fish with a side of slaw." Then I point to the menu on the wall. "I think it's number two up there."

We sit down at the table waiting for our order.

"You know," I couldn't help myself from teasing him, "that fuzz on your head almost makes you look bald. I'll bet she was offering that senior special to you."

We both started laughing. The service was slow, they got our order wrong, but we had a great time.

"How could he take you there?" My girlfriends were horrified.

"It was his company that was fun," I reminded them. "Who cares where we went."

I can tell you, however, that you won't see me there again with a younger man. There is always the drive through window if someone has another craving for fish. But, thank you, I have enough senior moments of my own without a young waitress at a fast food restaurant giving me another.

The Underwear Thief

Running late for work I am trying to find my bra so I can finish dressing. What could I have done with it? I thought I flung it into the side room as I went to take my shower. But maybe I was mistaken. Sometimes when I am rushed I am a little foggy on what I am doing. Ever have one of those episodes when you put something in a safe place, then the place is so safe that even you can't find it? That's how I am feeling at the moment.

This is not the first time I have missed something in the past few weeks. One day my bikini panties were nowhere to be found after I stepped out of a nice hot shower. A few nights later the T-shirt I sleep in vanished. It has a big yellow chicken wearing glasses printed on the front with the words *one smart chick*. Perhaps that one should have stayed missing. But I like wearing it to bed when I am alone and am reading. Two smart chicks in bed, one printed on my chest and the other laying on her butt with a book in front of her.

I did find them all, and some missing shoes in the living room. It seems I am the fashion victim of the newest member of the household who has been here all of three weeks. Bray.

Wrapped in my towel I slowly peek into the living room. Aha. Just what I thought. The underwear thief is at it again. He is currently sitting on his rug in front of the TV, my bra under him and the strap between his teeth. Chewing contently, oblivious to the world around him.

"NO!" I screech at him. His head turns in my direction and he drops my bra as he runs out of the room. I bend down holding my towel in place with one hand and swiping back my bra with the other. Ick. It is damp from his loving licks.

My new dog. Just saying those words makes me grin. Fur so black that when he smiles his little white teeth form an upside down crescent moon across the dark landscape of his face. A silly smile, but one that lets you know he is happy. Some days he looks at you with those tiny brown eyes of his wondering if you are friend or foe. Then the moment passes and he is relaxed and playful. Playful, but distant.

He is still frightened so I pace myself in correcting him when he is naughty. I can just barely touch him and I don't want a harsh word to make him pull away and retreat to his own dark world where humans are not so welcomed.

I thought my gentle ways were paying off, making him want something of mine close by him. My scent reminding him he is safe.

I have learned differently. My shy new dog has an underwear fetish.

The young man I see sometimes on Saturday night is coming over. A friend with benefits or a boyfriend? The question is never discussed. We play, we tease, we have fun. It is casual and works for me. I am not ready for anything serious.

He called me. "Wear something sexy Saturday night."

"You wear something sexy," my reply to him. I am smiling, knowing he will.

"Oh, yeah, I've got some black bikini briefs," he told me. "Never wear them, but for you I will."

He did wear them as I found out later that night. And may I say he looked as you would image a cute, thin, hard body young man would look in them. I guess I was not the only one eyeing his briefs.

In the bedroom, while making love by candlelight, I heard a slight prancing sound going around the bed. A tiny jingle of a chain and I knew in an instant, my new dog was up to something. It was not easy turning away from the attention I was getting, but I had to check out what Bray was doing.

There in the flickering glow of candlelight, just the hint of an outline of my dog and in his mouth my friend's black briefs. Bray stood in the doorway for just a minute. I saw the quick shake of his head and the briefs dangling on either side of his mouth. He turned quickly and danced down the hallway proud of his catch.

"Oh, God," I said to my friend as he was kissing my neck, "the dog just ran out with your briefs." In the blink of an eye my friend sat up, jumped off the bed and ran down the hall to retrieve his underwear.

I was amused with the dog's antics, but not sure how my friend would feel. Most men would not find Bray's actions as funny as I did.

He came back laughing, holding the damp briefs in his hand. Then he snuggled back down next to me. No harm, no foul, just a slight interruption. I like that he laughed about it.

I've never had a problem with dogs chewing on clothing or anything they shouldn't. But then my husband trained them. They knew he meant business when he said "no" and they listened to the master they adored.

I am the weak one. The one that kisses dogs and scolds them with the softest voice, then hands them a treat. When met with shredded magazines after arriving home from work, I take photos of the mess to share with my friends, laughing at the scene before me rather than disciplining the dogs.

I am sure the one trained here will be me. Dear Bray will continue to run off with things when I turn my back and I will be the one who learns to put my clothes out of his reach.

I am a failure at dog training and a gentle touch. My dogs know that. But for any man who enters these doors, beware, for there is an underwear thief on the prowl.

Someone New In My Bed

I am giddy. Finally a body to sleep with me every night. It was such an obvious solution to my wanting a bed partner, I almost missed it.

Another dog has joined the pack. Annabelle. She arrived at my house a few days ago. I had not planned on getting another dog so quickly after Bray. But I am not one that is good at sticking to a plan.

At first glance she is not much to look at. Part Hound dog, part Beagle. The rescue group that brought me Bray pulled her out of animal control in the nick of time. Her owners had turned her in saying they could not afford to keep her.

"Let me show you this sweet gal." I had gone over to look at another dog that was too wild for my timid crew and was about to get in my car and leave. "I'll be right back." This nice looking man was excited to bring me a substitute.

My first look at Annabelle made me turn away and want to run. She waddled out on the lawn, short stubby legs, tan color, short close fur, and over weight at 45 pounds. She did not show much interest in me either. She is missing enough teeth that when she looks at you and smiles her lips curl up inside her mouth. Reminds me of that character *Maxine*. Sourpuss would describe her at that moment. Her belly hangs low from years of puppies. And those are her good points. Add to that a heart murmur, skin allergies, and gum disease.

Not wanting to seem impolite I said, "Let me know how her vet visit goes." I put the incident behind me figuring Annabelle was out of the question. Surely something else was wrong with her and I wouldn't be able to take her in. Part of me hoped for that. *Shame on me*.

My cell rang two days later. "We're leaving the vets now and want to bring Annabelle by to see how she does with your other dogs."

"Is she OK?" I wanted to know how her check up went.

"Yeah, she's got a few issues, but minor. And she's older than we thought." It seems her previous owner said she was about five, but the vet put her age between 8 and 10. Guess the dog owners felt she would appeal more if she were younger. God does that younger gal thing apply to dogs as well as widows?

Still uncertain about Annabelle all I could say was, "Bring her over." After all I was the one who had contacted them in whatever moment went through my brain that day. Oh yes, I remember *why* now.

This is Foxy's fault I thought. Last week she was behaving oddly. She is thirteen and has joint problems. She was sleeping in the bedroom during the day, and Bray was guarding the door.

My first thought, she's dying. Ever the optimist, but it has been a tough year. Even my new dog was keeping an eye on her. Dog body language told me something was wrong.

Then I looked at Bray, close by her with his worried look. What if something did happen to Foxy? How would I handle Bray? He needs to be in the company of dogs. So that is how I wound up on the rescue site again. As soon as I made the call Foxy was suddenly up and active. Had I been duped by these two cunning canines?

I peeked out the front window as the van drove up. As soon as Annabelle's short stubby legs hit the ground the hellhounds started barking in the house.

The couple from Animal Action Rescue brought Annabelle to the kitchen door. I opened it and she walked in as if she owned the place. Went to check out every room with a casualness that was cool. Bray and Foxy followed her tails wagging with each step.

Annabelle turned to look at me. I had not noticed her big brown cow like eyes or her long lashes the other day. There was something pretty in that screwed up little face of hers. She looked at me to smile, for dogs do smile. Mine sure do. Her two canine teeth poking out of her bottom jaw caught the upper part of her mouth making her look like she'd been stung by a bee. Two big puff balls on either side of her mouth.

"Maybe she could spend the night?" Seemed like the next logical step. Annabelle had made herself at home and my heart was melting looking at her. I watched them drive off and knew their next trip over would be to pick up my check, not *my* Annabelle.

"Good girl." I bent over to pet her as she sat at my feet looking up at me with those soulful eyes. Her breath was killer, I would have to work on that.

I started to relax. Looking out across the room were three dogs looking back at me. All about the same size, yet all different. It was kind of fun.

That night when I went to bed I brought in a small rug for Annabelle to sleep on. I dropped it on the floor next to the spot Foxy has slept on for thirteen years. Bray sleeps in his crate, which he chooses to do. It is his safe house.

Annabelle looked at the small rug, dismissed it and waddled over to me. She placed her front paws up on the bed's edge, wiggled that plump rump of hers and gave me a questioning look.

I know what's on your mind, old gal. I smiled at her and patted the bed. She jumped up, snuggled next to me, rested her head on my shoulder and fell asleep. It has been a long time since I've had a bedmate and I loved the warmth of her chubby body close to mine.

One last look around me as I reached to turn off the light. Three dogs sleeping soundly can fill an empty room. I click off the light, turn to my side and gently place my arm over Annabelle, pulling her closer to me. An old dog to fill the empty void next to me in bed.

Oh God, will I ever have a date again with this crew in the bedroom? Annabelle nuzzles my arm and I kiss the top of her head. Who cares? I am gleefully happy with my new bedmate. My final thought as I drifted off for the best nights sleep I've had in a year.

It's A Jungle Out There

My jungle is different than the one Randy Newman sings about on one of my favorite TV shows *Monk*. My jungle is my back yard. Full of animals and critters I never saw when I was married. Now I see everything moving, slinking about in my yard. My husband, exterminator aka terminator, kept bugs and critters at bay. You could find him on spring days in his jeans, a long denim shirt, a bandana and a respirator spraying the foundation of the house, the crawl space and the attic. We had no bugs then.

Me, I am a target for anything that crawls or flies into my yard. I don't spray anything. I am of the old school, if I see it move I stomp it with my foot. If I see it crawling up the wall, I whack it with my hand. And if I am not quick enough and a roach crawls across the floor, Foxy pounces on it.

The light fixture in my kitchen is full of bodies. It is too heavy for me to remove and clean, so every night I look at it and shudder. Another moth has flown in the screen door to the light and fried. One day I will get a friend to help me take it down and shake out all the bugs that have been seduced by its glow and ended their lives in my kitchen light. In the meantime I try to ignore the shadows of their tiny bodies when I turn the light on.

Ants have been crawling the brick wall by the kitchen door. They have now migrated into the kitchen and hang around my sink looking for tasty morsels. I thought I had them under control. *Whack, whack, whack* and a hundred died in an instant under the palm of my hand. But no, they are back again.

The biggest insult of all, ants are crawling on my Corvette. I walk out and see them marching in lines across the white hood of my car. They leave my van alone. So I am guessing I have muscle ants rather than soccer ants.

"Yeah, they're all over my car too," my best friend tells me. "I've sprayed the inside of my car, but they are still there."

"Well thank goodness they are not inside my car. But I hate this." I complain back.

Walking my dogs in the back yard is a blood sacrifice. Mosquitoes bite me. They are everywhere too.

"You need to fence in the yard for the dogs," my best friend keeps telling me now that I have three. "Just open the door and let them out. You don't have to worry."

"What about the bugs and critters?" I asked her. I am worried my dogs will be devoured by nature's beasts in my yard.

"They are dogs, silly," she chided me. "They'll love the freedom of being able to play. And you can relax they are fenced in."

She's right. The three try to romp in the yard, but I have them leashed.

So I make the call for my fence. It is simple really, three sides are already fenced. A hundred feet of chain link will solve my problem. Why couldn't I figure this out myself?

This year nature has been terrorizing me. That's why. I am finding bodies all over my yard. Dead rats, dead moles, and a slinking live snake. I am not comfortable with all of that in my yard and the thought of letting my dogs roam freely. I am never sure what Annabelle sees. But I can see her, butt up in the air diving at something in the ivy. Then there are the bees and wasps. I am worried for my dogs' safety.

Now I have my own Killer Cicada Wasp flying in my yard. I

noticed a large mound of dirt with a hole in it right off the back patio. At the very moment my eye saw the hole, a huge black and yellow insect flew out of it.

I jumped in horror. "Come on, let's go." I yell at the dogs and we all run to the back door.

I called the Reverend. "I've got something building a nest under ground. What do I do?" I was sure we were in grave danger.

"Yes ma'm," he chuckled on the phone, "most likely a yellow jacket nest. Them are mean fella's."

He told me you kill the nest at night, pour gas down the hole and light it up. "They don't fly at night. You don't want to mess with it at day."

Well it was already nightfall and I was too tired to deal with it. *Tomorrow*, I thought. My Scarlett mentality since I am on my own.

The next morning when I went out the hole was gone, but the mound was still there. As I stood looking in confusion at the dirt the bee flew past me again. It was about two inches long, black and yellow and looked ominous at best. *Too big to be a yellow jacket* my little bit of bug knowledge told me.

What was it? I Googled and found my answer. *Eastern cicada killer wasp*. Named that, not because it kills people, but because it hunts cicadas for its nests. They are the largest wasps seen in the United States. And now I have one in my yard. Perfect.

I read further. My killer bee is a solitary female wasp going about her family business. The female captures the cicada paralyzing it with a sting, then deposits it in the nest for food for the young. The cicada is often twice the size as the wasp, and there are photos online showing a wasp with her cicada crawling into a human hand for help. After depositing the cicada in the hole, a few eggs are laid and then the wasp exits closing the hole allowing the eggs to feed on the cicada.

The male has no stinger and the female is not aggressive, she rarely stings. I was amazed at what I read. Suddenly I felt pleased to have her busy in my yard. I have no idea what to expect from all the work she is doing, but I guess time will tell.

I am keeping an eye on my Cicada Killer Wasp. The solitary female who is busy every day, working hard to make nests for her eggs. She buzzes about my yard alone, planning for the future with diligence and hard work. She does not fear the humans who are close by, so I should not fear her. My jungle of a yard teaching me how to let nature take its course and relax with the flow of life. My fence goes in tomorrow.

My Ever Faithful Male

I look back over the last year and one man stands out above the rest. It has taken me until today to realize how much he has meant to me and how his appearance at my front door pulled me out of my sorrow every time he knocked.

How did I ever overlook him? My god, he has been there for me since the day after my husband's death. I am embarrassed I took him so for granted.

I call him when I am lonely and he always appears.

When I am sad he brings something that pleases.

If I am tired he makes sure I don't have to cook.

I never worry that he will stand me up.

He lets me make my own decisions and never says *no*.

I can choose what I want he doesn't criticize.

He always greets me with a big smile.

He likes it when I have a party and doesn't mind a group.

I can share him with others, but he is always there for me too.

He has his own transportation and knows when to leave.

He is the one I am always anxious to see.

His knock on my front door is the most welcomed of all.

Forgive me for taking so long to say *thanks*.

My dear Dominos Pizza delivery man.

A Garden of Memories

Here's the dirt. *Don't tell on me.* I work at a Botanical Garden and my house is full of fake flowers. While most gardeners are weeding, trying out the newest green way to get rid of insects, I am out looking for silk flower dust spray. I have a huge yard but my joy of gardening is found in my house.

My walls are my blooming garden, my tribute to nature. Every room is full of vintage floral paintings. Every flower you can think of is blooming in a painting throughout my house. The expensive paintings and my thrift store finds blend together as beautifully as any flowers that grow outdoors.

I have a vintage concrete garden statue collection that stays indoors. I love my rooms to look like you walked into a cottage garden. Old crusty cement pots filled with lovely pale orchids fill every corner. Tiny violets spill out of hand painted clay pots, thrift store finds that some child most likely decorated. They line my cupboard shelves. Frog garden statues, old and new sit on tables holding up stacks of old garden books. The flowers are all artificial. I would not be able to keep up with them if they weren't.

It's almost embarrassing that I love these flowers so much. They add sparkle to every niche and I never have to water them. "I have a drought free garden," I brag. I just wish it were dust free.

Many years ago a dear friend came to visit. She hated artificial flowers, but was drawn to the lovely rose bouquet on my dining room table. It looked so real, with its little dewdrop on a petal, she walked over to smell its delightful fragrance. For surely these magical roses must smell divine.

"Oh, God," I could hear the grimace in her voice. "Shit, these are fake." She turned at me looking completely disgusted. "What's the point?" And then, if I remember correctly, she sneezed from the dust.

The point is that they looked so real she tried to smell them. Now that is a pretty good fake arrangement.

My husband disliked my fake flowers too. I had lovely artificial Geraniums tucked in baskets in the sunroom. He would look at the fake red blossoms and shake his head. "Do you have to have these?"

"Why yes, I do. They give the room color." I held my ground.

An old real estate buddy of his stopped by one afternoon to pick up some papers. They had to pass the sunroom to get to my husband's office. The guy saw my fake Geraniums, looked at my husband and so help me these words came out of his mouth. "Wow, look at those flowers. Now someone here has a green thumb."

My fake flowers were never questioned again.

I love real flowers, don't get me wrong. My house is a tribute to my love of gardens and flowers. Just not in quite the traditional way most folks think of.

My yard on the other hand is special because of its memories. When I sit outside on the old wood bench my husband built and look out at the expanse of lawn, my old life smiles back to me. Every flowerbed holds something dear to me, more precious than the plants that grow there.

There is a history in that garden. Boy's old blue Frisbee still rests next to the garden bench looking as if Boy might come play at any time. I look across the lawn and remember my husband's tall lean body turning gracefully as he pitched the Frisbee to Boy, the dog that would not tire chasing it.

Boy's huge cement marker is now covered thick with ivy. But I know it is there.

Jake is buried in the yard too. A stepping stone with the words *Big Dogs Are Best* marks his spot. He was that big dog I could rest my head on. In the distance the tulip tree is starting to bloom. One of my favorite photos of Jake was taken under that tree. He is looking at the camera and the pink and white blossoms surround his head like big saucers. Jake, so photogenic, is now Mr. February in the 2010 German Shepherd Rescue of North Carolina calendar.

My husband loved elephant ears and every spring he would beat me to the planters to fill them with his bulbs that had been stored carefully in paper bags over the winter.

"No," I would whine. "I wanted that spot for my rosemary."

He would gleefully chuckle that he got one up on me. "You snooze you loose."

Last winter I did not pull the bulbs but to my amazement they survived over the cold months. The elephant ears are pushing through the dirt and a few of the huge leaves have started to unroll. I smile as I look at them. I am sure somewhere my husband is grinning that somehow, yet again, he beat me to the planters.

I love my garden of memories as much as any gardener who works the soil. My dogs and I like to go into the yard when the weather is good. They are a frenzy of activity chasing each other, cutting through the flowerbeds that are blooming again, no thanks to me. I watch them and laugh. No, I am not planting anything in the yard again this year, but I am growing new memories every season.

A Window Fell On My Head

It is a simple thing, really. I went to open the window in the back bedroom to let in some fresh air. I pushed the window up and stuck my head in just a bit to adjust the storm window. *Bang!* The window dropped smack dab on the top of my head. Having just recently read of an actress who fell, hit her head and died, I immediately wondered if perhaps I would go into a coma in the next few minutes. I know, I know, a little dramatic. But this happened just at the stroke of midnight and now it is the first of May and it would have been our sixth wedding anniversary. I am wondering if perhaps my husband is calling and a knock on the head will take me to him. Hard to believe I actually had such a lovely day today and at midnight I am sounding morbid. But it is not really morbid, it is more of a passing thought, one of remembering that I was married six years ago and now I am a widow.

Yesterday morning while I was bringing in the e-mails, a note from Outlook popped up with an Anniversary reminder. It startled me so I jumped in my chair. My husband was wishing me *Happy Anniversary*. My sign from beyond! I sat there looking at the screen and said out loud, "Happy Anniversary to you too, hon."

He programmed that reminder right after we got married and it will continue to appear each year unless I cancel it. I left it scheduled because I think next year I would like to hear from him again.

My head hurts a little, but most likely I will be here to continue my life. I have a long workday ahead of me tomorrow, which will ease the fact I have no one to celebrate this day with. I don't want to be one of those widows that years down the road will say *well today would have been my wedding anniversary*. There is plenty of time to let it go, but this is my first anniversary without him and it feels good to remember.

I had two anniversary greetings actually. My girlfriend with the Spanish moss hair called while I was finishing my coffee to give me the other.

"Are you doing OK today? I know it would have been your anniversary." Then she panicked. I could hear it in her voice. "I'm not upsetting you am I?"

"No, I'm fine." I reassured her. I was actually so pleased she had the courage to call me and say that. Some of my friends were afraid to bring it up. But remembering my wedding made me happy.

Our wedding took place in the blink of an eye. After almost 20 years of living together we decided to get married, quietly, at the courthouse. I was more nervous than he was. It was a simple ceremony with a tiny female judge who looked up at my 6' 7" husband with delight. He had that effect on women, especially older woman. In two minutes we were married, so easy you would wonder why we didn't do it earlier. I do know that I was so happy to finally have that question out of the way. *Should we marry?*

I think I was afraid it would change us. We had a routine that worked and since he was so head strong I was worried he would take over and then it wouldn't work. How silly that all seems now. He was always the one for me. He knew it too, although he liked to kid me a bit on that.

"Yep, you moved in, bags and all two weeks after we met." That is really pretty close to the truth. If I was a canine, you could say I marked my territory.

An antique buddy of mine caught up with us at Kroger shortly after we got married. She cornered my husband and looked him square in the eye. "So what made you decide to get married finally?"

His answer to her, "I wanted to get married ten years earlier. She's the one." Then he nodded in my direction. It always charmed me that he said that because he was not outwardly romantic.

We weren't to tell anyone we were getting married. I cheated and told my mother because I was visiting her in Florida the weekend before. My sister was home for a few months from the Virgin Islands and they both knew. Mother sent me home with her wedding band and my dad's wedding band. My sister danced around me gleefully singing "Going To The Chapel And We're Gonna Get Married."

"Shhhhh," I said. "No one is to know!" But I can't keep a secret from my mother and my sister was there to overhear.

My best friend was out of town and that was good. I just wanted it to be the two of us so we could react the way we wanted without any outside influence. After twenty years I was nervous.

We had lunch before the ceremony, since we had a few hours wait for the judge. It was a sweet romantic lunch in downtown Decatur, across from the courthouse. We savored every moment knowing that we were about to do something extraordinary.

Our wedding evening was almost like any other. After the ceremony we went home, changed into jeans and went to drop off a few things at the antique shop then to get groceries.

"Let's go to Costco for steaks." My husband loved Costco. An event worthy of a celebration meant a 40 mile trip to go pick up steaks and wine. He loved to cook rather than eat out. Why fight it? The man could grill a steak.

So after all those years of living together we were married. Quickly, quietly and happily. I did not take his name but kept my own. Which was not my maiden name, but my first husband's name which I had never changed. My husband would tell people, "My wife has another man's name." Then he'd shake his head and laugh his hearty laugh. People were confused on how to address mail to us.

We didn't combine our finances and we continued our day-to-day living as always. Just the way we had wanted it. Nothing changed except that I loved the fact we were married. I don't know why I had worried so about it.

I was happy we were married when he got sick for I was able to be there to fight the battle with him with the doctors, not as a girl-friend, but as his wife. That was comforting in its own fashion. I do know that if he had died and we were never married I would have regretted that for the rest of my life. At least by finally marrying, the world knew we loved each other and took that vow. Better late than never.

So Happy Anniversary, honey. Thank you for the time of my life.

You Are Cordially Invited....

The vacuum is humming as I am sucking all the dog hair off the carpet. The fridge is packed with wine and beer. My musician friend, Larry Joe Hall, a great songwriter and guitarist, will be here this afternoon to set up his amps. Music will float through the night air later this evening when my friends arrive. I am a little frantic. Running behind schedule. So what is new with that? Some things never change.

But change is in the air. I am having a party.

I called one of my computer savvy friends. "How do I send an e-vite?" I want to send my invitations online with my computer.

"You are such a techno-phobe," he laughed at me. "Just Google e-vite and you'll find one to use." There was a slight pause, "Why are you asking? Don't tell me you are finally having a party."

"Yes, and you're invited. But you'll have to wait for your e-vite for the details." I hate to have him get one up on me.

My friends know I have not entertained in my house in a year. I used Jake as my excuse, can't have company over with a sick stinky dog. But he was my cover story. I wasn't ready to let anyone in my private safe house. Only when he died did I let a few people come through my doors. Certainly nothing like a group having a party.

"It's time." I told my best friend.

May has come full circle and is staring me in the face. "Back at ya May." I can smile finally and breathe in the lovely spring air without fear.

May. How can one month hold so many memories? I met my

husband in May, we married in May and he died in May. Now, my first party since being a widow, is in May. I will never look at May with anything other than awe.

My husband's cousin and her husband are visiting from Indiana. So they are my guests of honor so to speak. She actually took charge of the house getting things in order for I am not known for my cleaning skills, only my decorating style. I haven't seen a book on my particular style yet, so maybe that will be next on my list of things to do. Vintage charm meets thrift store crap and the results are simply fabu.

"Where are your cleaning supplies?" She had marched into the kitchen earlier just as I poured my first cup of coffee.

"Why?" That cleaning word alien to me. A word that makes me tremble with fear. "Not sure I have much."

"Well that bathroom is a mess. I'm going to scrub it down and need some cleaner for the tub."

"No one is going to take a bath tonight, can't we just close the shower door?" My cleaning tips for those who are lazy like myself.

I saw her hands on her hips and heard a little tapping sound on the floor. Oh my, she is serious. My house seems clean to me, but then perhaps I am not the best judge of that. I live with dogs and am used to their standards.

"I'm heading out shortly for extra wine and I'll pick something up," I whined back to her.

"Get those Clorox tablets for the john too"

"What is that for?"

"Don't you ever use them? Great for keeping the john perky white." Now here is valuable information. I'm game.

After all, she gave me the bra lecture yesterday. "If you own several bras you don't have to keep waiting for the wash and if your dog steals one, you've got a second." I only own one. How did I live so long without this knowledge?

"Where is my frog?" I yelled out the bathroom door. I have a huge cement frog on the bathroom counter and he is missing.

"I put him under the sink so you can put out hand towels for your guests."

"No way." I am mostly muttering this to myself. He is my bathroom mascot and will sit proudly by the sink. The hand towels can rest in a basket nearby. I pulled him back out to his place of honor. "Such a handsome frog." I speak to him like he can hear. Stranger things have happened. I kiss him gently on the top of his head; after all, you never know what frog will suddenly emerge as your prince.

As I turn in the doorway she is standing there eyeing the frog.

"Don't touch him," I warn her, then start giggling and give her a hug.

She and her husband are the best. We have had several days sitting on the patio laughing about my husband and all the crazy things he did as a kid, when she knew him and I didn't.

"Remember that night we played *You Don't Know Jack* on the computer?" She has just brought up one of the visits they made to see us some years back. Her comments snapping me back to the present.

When I think about my old life I wonder if things will ever be that simple again. We were not so young when we met in our mid thirties, but young enough to have had a history that can never be repeated. Parents, friends, and the enthusiasm of doing whatever it took to be together, to make it work. Growing with each other for 25 years and taking for granted that love would always be there.

My old life I can now think about and smile. My memories

tender not painful.

The house reflects the new me and I have filled it full of my favorite things. Small personal items of my husband's tucked carefully away, treasures I can't part with. His modern furniture gone, replaced by my old worn pieces.

The only piece of furniture I kept was the sofa he died on. How strange is that? I hated that sofa when he bought it the month we met. A big Italian modern wide arm sofa in a taupe color fabric that is velvety to the touch. I still don't like it. But it is as comfortable as the day he bought it and it has been Foxy's bed for thirteen years. I've tossed a few vintage patchwork quilts on it disguising its manliness and it has its charm.

You would think that would have been the first to go when I went on my rampage redecorating the house to keep my sanity. Truth is I like to lie on it and think of him. Not of the night he died, but of all the years we snuggled on this couch watching TV. There is plenty of time down the road to find a new couch. I am not ready to part with the memories of this one.

The girl I used to be? She has met up to the woman I have become. I am now a mixture of all my selves. I am that adventuresome gal who fell in love at first sight when I met my future husband and took that daring leap of faith. I am still the good wife and hold dear to my heart my husband's memories, the goodness of our life together and all that being a couple taught me. And finally, a widow, the word I hate, replaced with a new word that I am enjoying. *Woman*.

I can't wait to listen to the music tonight. I'm ready. I've learned that you need to hold on to the best of what was in your life to make good of what is yet to come.

A good friend over dinner one evening said to me, "We all have our stories, your husband lived his, yours is still continuing."

Such a simple sentence but filled with the truth. A year ago I sat on the couch crying and lost. "What will I do, how will I fill my time, how can I go on?" A year later I have so much to do I worry how I will have time to get it done. It amazes me that a new life has been created. My life. A small bright rainbow at the end of my tears.

Heavy Petting Again

Snuggled on the couch next to a new male I am back to my old tricks. Heavy petting. Never met a male who didn't respond to a gentle caress and this one is no exception.

My dog Bray. The timid boy, playful, but unapproachable, is now by my side letting me run my hands through his fur. His head tilts up as I gently rub his neck. Two months ago I couldn't do this. He was still too frightened from his past demons. Now he comes to me wanting more.

"Good boy." I whisper close to his face, then drop a gentle kiss on his nose. He lets me do this. I am thrilled. My love of dogs is never ending. I am happier having a rescue dog come out of his shell then having a man come out of his pants. Is there any hope for me?

We have finally bonded. He prances up to me now, his smile full of devilish fun, wanting to be petted. He pushes through my female dogs to claim his share of attention. We started with a gentle touch and now he loves my heavy petting.

I look at the trio of dogs before me and smile. They are my family now when I come home at night. The sounds of their barking escalate as my car hits the driveway and I am anxious to join them. Once again there is a house full of love to greet me as I turn the key.

My dogs keep my heart open. They make me laugh. They show me how love can bring you out of yourself. That love can overcome trauma. They teach me that patience and caring are two important ingredients to form any relationship, human or animal. Bray has reminded me that a broken spirit can be mended. My own spirit soars when I am with the pack. A riot of heavy petting, wet kisses and joy.

"Three dogs, are you crazy?" I hear this a lot from friends and strangers.

My answer. "I'd be crazy without them."

Dogs teach me that no matter how sad I get love is always within reach. Bray has come out of his shell, but he, Foxy and Annabelle have brought me out of mine.

Today I am petting my dogs with abandon, we will see what tomorrow brings. For heavy petting has always been a favorite pastime of mine.

Dear God, We've Only Just Begun

Dear God,

By golly, you did. We did it. There is a life before my eyes that is shaping up nicely. I am not ready for you to stop your magic, but I am pleased with our progress.

In a year's time I have found myself again. I am not complete by any means, but who really ever is? Everyday an opportunity to learn, to grow, to become the person I am meant to be. To be the person you have in mind for me to be. Maybe even a successful writer if you liked our adventures this year.

You have sent me answers with the strangest messengers. I go to a dating service to meet men and come away with a car, a job and a writing class. I have met new friends that have enriched my life. I now have a bevy of dogs that helped me become my old self again. You know, that old self that cries on occasion but now laughs with joy and cracks jokes all the time.

With your help I have stopped dwelling on my own drama and try to help others with theirs. That old caregiver I used to be peeking out again able to give back to others.

This is not our final conversation. You know what a talker I am.

Sincerely, Barbara
Formally known as the Widow Barbara

PS – This new dog Chloe, the seven-pound two-year-old fawn colored Chihuahua that just came home with me from the animal shelter, what is that about? Four dogs now, instead of three. Is that in your plan for me? Or am I just a sucker for a sweet face and a wagging tail?

Redefine The Impossible.

I like to think I rescued dogs,
but the truth is that they have rescued me.

Thanks To My Rescue Folks:
Animal Action Rescue, Decatur, Georgia
www.animalactionrescue.org

Atlanta Canine Adoption Project, Atlanta, Georgia
www.petfinder.com/shelters/GA244.html

To The Vets Who Look After My Dogs:
North Dekalb Veterinary Clinic, Decatur, Georgia
www.northdekalbvet.com

Loving Touch Animal Center, Stone Mountain, Georgia
www.lovingtouchac.com

And A Pet Sitter Every Gal Needs:
www.petmeisters.com

Coming Sooner Or Later!

Covered In Fur, Lessons Learned Living With Six Dogs
by Barbara Barth, copyright 2010

What do you do when you can't get a date for New Year's Eve?
Get a dog. Maybe two. My pack went from four dogs to
six thanks to one margarita and a call to my local shelter.

The last male in these doors made a hasty retreat.
"Those dogs are giving me a headache."

_Oh my._

Visit me at my web!
www.barbarabarth.net

As always, covered in fur,
but surrounded by love.
Barbara

LaVergne, TN USA
25 April 2010
180439LV00001B/1/P